In Christ are hidden all the treasures of wisdom and knowledge (Col. 2:3). To Francis Frangipane, God has given unparalleled abilities to mine out that gold in ways that enrich all of us beyond measure. Rarely do I ever read even one paragraph from my dear friend that I don't feel like saying, "I was blind, but now I see." *The Shelter of the Most High* will take you places you've never gone before in your walk with Jesus, truly experiencing Him as your supreme shelter.

—David Bryant
Founder, Concerts of Prayer International and
President, PROCLAIM HOPE!
Author of *Christ Is All!*

Where do you find shelter in the midst of a violent storm? What do you do when the battle rages and your strength is all but gone? How do you hear God's voice above the thunder of intense spiritual warfare? Who can help when you're blind-sided by an unforeseen tragedy? Francis Frangipane has, once again, heard from God and points the way in *The Shelter of the Most High*. The principles found throughout this book are ageless and will be an enduring encouragement to the reader for years to come.

—Steve Hill
Pastor and Evangelist
Dallas, Texas

With stunning clarity, Francis Frangipane has brought forth another jewel from his treasury of Christlike wisdom in *The Shelter of the Most High*. Need encouragement for your journey? Need insight from the Word of God? Then go no further. Francis has done it again! Read and learn how you can dwell in the secret place of the Most High!

—Dr. James W. Goll
Cofounder, Encounters Network; Director, Prayer Storm
Author of *The Seer, Angelic Encounters, The Lost Art of Intercession, Praying for Israel's Destiny,* and many more

For several years, the Lord has kept me studying the vast amount of biblical material on God's house as a place of refuge and intimacy for believers today. So, it was with great joy and much encouragement that I read Francis Frangipane's new presentation *The Shelter of the Most High*. We will all profit from the insight gleaned by this wise teacher of Scriptural truth.

—Dave Butts
President, Harvest Prayer Ministries
Chairman, National Prayer Committee

The Shelter
of the
Most High

The Shelter
of the
Most High

F R A N C I S
F R A N G I P A N E

Charisma
HOUSE
A STRANG COMPANY

Design Director: Bill Johnson
Cover Designer: Karen Grindley

Library of Congress Cataloging-in-Publication Data:

Frangipane, Francis.
  The shelter of the most high / Francis Frangipane.
     p. cm.
  ISBN 978-1-59979-281-1
  1. Suffering--Religious aspects--Christianity. I. Title.

  BV4909.F73 2008
  248.8'6--dc22

                                    2008010448

08 09 10 11 12 — 987654321
Printed in the United States of America

Contents

I love You, O LORD, my strength.

The LORD is my rock and my fortress and my deliverer,

My God, my rock, in whom I take refuge;

My shield and the horn of my salvation, my stronghold.

I call upon the LORD, who is worthy to be praised,

And I am saved from my enemies.

—Psalm 18:1–3

INTRODUCTION

THE BIBLE WARNS of the time before Christ's return when Satan shall be cast to the earth. The devil, in ever-increasing rage, will come, "...having great wrath, knowing that he has only a short time" (Rev. 12:12). While many search to know the specific timing of this event, one thing is obvious: in today's world, evil has become more aggressive than ever.

Thus it is imperative that we who have set our hearts on Christ learn how to abide in the living presence of God. For it is only in Him that we find the place of safety from the increasing darkness.

When I speak of protection, however, I do not mean that while on Earth we will escape suffering. Many will face persecution and even death for Jesus's sake, as the Scriptures warn: "All who...live godly in Christ Jesus will be persecuted" (2 Tim. 3:12). Nor should we expect to find a spiritual reality where we are so *spiritual* that the world finally loves us. If the enemies of God hated Jesus, they will hate us as well (John 15:18–19). Yet there *is* a place of immunity. It is here, in the shelter of the Most High, where the Lord bids us to abide.

Let me also emphasize that we do not need unusual, personal conflict to desire to abide in the presence of God. Vision compelled by hunger can take us there. Worship and a pure heart can lift us Godward. Yet whether we are driven toward the stronghold of God because of problems or passion, there is a holy place where the divine presence becomes our shelter.

Once we have found this secret place in God, nothing we encounter in life can truly defeat us; God Himself preserves us in all things. In every distress or devilish plot aligned against us, we emerge as "more than conquerors" (Rom. 8:37, KJV). In God's shelter, the redemptive power of Christ reverses the plans of Satan, annulling both the assault of the enemy and its aftereffects.

Beloved, even now you may be in a place of isolation, fear, or defeat. Yet your current condition is not a limitation to the Almighty. From where you are, you can reach the place of spiritual immunity: the shelter of the Most High.

—Francis Frangipane

God is our refuge and strength,

A very present help in trouble.

Therefore we will not fear, though the earth should change

And though the mountains slip into the heart of the sea;

Though its waters roar and foam,

Though the mountains quake at its swelling pride. Selah.

There is a river whose streams make glad the city of God,

The holy dwelling places of the Most High.

God is in the midst of her, she will not be moved;

God will help her when morning dawns.

The nations made an uproar, the kingdoms tottered;

He raised His voice, the earth melted.

The LORD of hosts is with us;

The God of Jacob is our stronghold. Selah.

—Psalm 46:1–7

ONE

WHERE A DESOLATE SOUL FINDS GOD

JESUS GAVE THE last hours of this age a poignant head-line. He called this period "the Great Tribulation." The word rendered *tribulation* means "grievous afflic-tion or distress; pressure or burden upon the spirit." As we move closer toward the end of this age, we should expect that catastrophic distresses and pressures on man shall increase.

Added to the increasing stress of our times is the decreasing desire of government and society in general to restrain moral decadence. We live in a time when a significant portion of our society is in open and defiant rebellion toward God. The prophetic words of Psalm 2 are being fulfilled before our eyes: World and local leaders "take their stand and the rulers take counsel together against the LORD and against His Anointed" (v. 2). As they renounce moral values, their militant cry is, "Let us tear their fetters apart and cast away their cords from us!" (v. 3).

Jesus warned of this day, saying, "Because lawlessness will abound, the love of many will grow cold" (Matt. 24:12, NKJV). If you are one who has resisted the increasing darkness, you know how intense and multifaceted the battle is. Whether you are fighting to remedy an injustice in your community or just trying to keep your family together, barely do we make headway in one area before five other areas are breeched.

In spite of breakthroughs occurring in several cities, many good people have grown weary. They are just going through the motions. The prophet Daniel warned of a time when the enemy would "…wear down the saints of the Highest One" (Dan. 7:25). To emerge victorious in this day, we must climb into the reality given to us by God in Psalm 91. There is place of replenishing life—a fountain of eternal life where we can abide. The Bible calls this place the shelter of the Most High.

ELIJAH: A MAN LIKE US

Elijah was a man with passions like ours, and he fought in a spiritual war similar to ours. In his battle for the soul of Israel, he stood against the wiles of Jezebel and her husband, King

Ahab. Yet his most intense battle was not against visible foes but against personal discouragement.

As bold as Elijah was, he lived as a fugitive, moving in and out of caves and places of hiding. Jezebel had murdered nearly all of the Lord's prophets, replacing their godly influence with the dark, satanic oppression accompanying the priests of Baal and the Asherah. A new initiative, however, had come from the Lord: Both Elijah and the prophets of Baal were to build altars, each to the deity they individually served. The God who answered with fire would be acknowledged as Lord over the nation.

King Ahab and all Israel came to the confrontation. Try as they may, the priests of Baal could draw no response from their demonic idol, Baal. In dramatic contrast, at Elijah's prayer, fire immediately fell from heaven and consumed his sacrifice. This was Elijah's greatest victory. And when the Israelites saw the display of God's power, they bowed to the ground, saying, "The LORD, He is God; the LORD, He is God" (1 Kings 18:39).

But the Lord was not finished. After Elijah had the priests of Baal executed, he went to the top of Mount Carmel, and, kneeling face down, he prayed seven times for rain until the Lord brought a great downpour that ended a devastating three-year drought. On this one day, both fire and rain miraculously fell from heaven!

Elijah had offered the Lord his very best effort. Yet, like the prophets before him, Elijah could not trigger revival for Israel. Discouragement overwhelmed him.

Perhaps if this tremendous day had occurred at almost any other time in Israel's history, the nation would have repented, but it did not. Baal worship should have ended, but it continued. In fact, nothing changed. Instead of the revival that Elijah envisioned, the opposite occurred: an enraged Jezebel vowed to kill the Lord's prophet, spurring Elijah to flee into the wilderness. There Elijah collapsed, exhausted and despondent, beneath a juniper tree. "It is enough; now, O Lord," the weary prophet prayed, "take my life, for I am not better than my fathers" (1 Kings 19:4).

Elijah had offered the Lord his very best effort. This day had been the culminating event of his life. Elijah had prayed that Israel would know the Lord was their God and that, in response, the Lord would turn Israel's "heart back again" (1 Kings 18:37). Yet, like the prophets before him, Elijah could not trigger revival for Israel. Discouragement overwhelmed him. He had had enough.

Have you been to the point of spiritual or emotional exhaustion where you too have said, "It is enough"? Perhaps you were frustrated by your own inability to effect positive change in your family or you've fasted and prayed for your church or society but no visible change occurred. You gave your all but found little success. Disheartened and weary like Elijah, all your resources were spent.

Elijah lay down and slept. As he did, an angel touched him and said, "Arise, eat" (1 Kings 19:5). At his head were bread and water. Elijah, weary with life itself, ate and withdrew back into sleep.

Once more the angel touched him. "Arise," he said. "Eat, because the journey is too great for you" (v. 7). For all our visions, plans, and programs, the journey before each of us is also "too great." Indeed our journey is divinely designed to be too great for us. The Lord has no plan where we succeed without Him. Life is so constructed to drive us to God.

BACK TO OUR FOUNDATIONS

So [Elijah] arose and ate and drank, and went in the strength of that food forty days and forty nights to Horeb, the mountain of God.

—1 Kings 19:8

The Lord gave Elijah strength, not to send him back to battle but to bring him back to basics. If we become more consumed with our task than we are with our love for God, our lives will eventually become brittle and desolate. To restore our souls, the Lord brings us back to the essentials of our faith. Indeed, He might even stop our labors completely and direct us to the simpler realities of prayer, time in the Word, and worship. He reminds us that, of all He calls us to accomplish, His greatest commandment is to love

Him with all our "heart…soul…mind…and…strength" (Mark 12:30). Without this focus, we lose touch with God's presence; we are outside the shelter of the Most High.

The Lord brought Elijah to "Horeb, the mountain of God." In Hebrew, *Horeb* means "desolation."* The barren environment mirrored Elijah's soul. Yet to God, Horeb was actually a place where the issues of a man's heart were flushed to the surface. There is no theater at Horeb, no acting. It is the place of unembellished honesty and core-to-surface transparency.

How Did You Get Here?

Perhaps Elijah's greatest virtue was his zeal. Indeed, twice in his communication with God, Elijah speaks of having been "very zealous" for the Lord. But zeal unaccompanied by wisdom eventually becomes its own god. It compels us toward expectations that are unrealistic and outside the timing and anointing of the Lord.

To remain balanced, zeal must be reined in and harnessed by strategic encounters with the living God. Otherwise we become frustrated with people and discouraged with delays. We step outside our place of strength and spiritual protection.

Elijah had come to Horeb and lodged there in a cave. Soon the Word of the Lord came to him: "What are you doing here, Elijah?" (v. 9). This is one of the most important questions God will ever ask us. His question probes the reality of our spiritual state: "How did your service to Me become dry and desolate?"

---

* Hebrew: *Charab*—to make desolate

God wants us to know that when we fail to esteem Him as our first love, we will always find a desert awaiting us.

Our primary purpose in life must be to abide in Christ. Otherwise we can become so consumed with the deteriorating condition of the world that we fail to see the deteriorating condition of our own soul. In His love, the Lord stops us and forces us to look honestly at our heart: Is this existence that I now live the abundant life promised me from Christ?

> One of the most important questions God will ever ask is: "How did your service to Me become dry and desolate?" God wants us to know that when we fail to esteem Him as our first love, we will always find a desert awaiting us.

Let's speak candidly. We have nothing to prove and no need to pretend. We can abandon the internal mechanisms of defensiveness and pride. If we are disappointed, we are free to express it; if frustrated, we can admit it. We must simply and truthfully evaluate, without rationalization, our true spiritual condition.

Lord, reveal to me my heart. Bring to the surface of my consciousness those disappointments and heartaches, as well as my sins and failures. Remove the cargo of oppression from my soul. Help me, Master, to lie still as You perform heart surgery on me.

Transparency is the outer garment of humility, and humility draws the grace of God to our hearts. Is not intimacy with God the very thing we most neglect? And is not the Lord alone our source of strength in battle? If the enemy can distract us from our time alone with God, he will isolate us from the help that comes from God alone.

Let us, therefore, approach the living God without any garment but with transparency.

A Fresh Anointing

As the pressures of this age escalate, we will soon discover that yesterday's anointing will not suffice for today's battles. The Lord brought a new beginning to Elijah's life at Horeb—one that would ultimately release a "double portion" of power to Elijah's successor, Elisha. Under this new anointing, Jezebel would be destroyed, Baal worship abolished, and the only period of revival the northern tribes ever experienced would begin.

To reach a similar place of breakthrough, it will take more than the momentum of our own zeal. We should not be surprised if God calls us to pass through our own Horeb.

How will we recognize this place? Horeb is the voice of personal desolation; it is the desperate compelling of our heart to possess more of God. We must now listen carefully to the voice of God. For it is at Horeb that He brings us deeper into Himself. It is here, under the canopy of His compassion, that we discover the purpose of our brokenness: *our desolation is, in fact, a time of preparation.*

The Lord is about to bring a new beginning to you. When

you return to the battle, you shall war from the shelter of the Most High.

Lord Jesus, apart from You my life is dry and desolate. Forgive me for trying to do Your will without abiding in Your presence. I desperately need You, Lord. This day, I commit my heart to return to my first love. Teach me, Lord, to consider intimacy with You the greatest measure of my success. Let me see Your glory; reveal to me Your goodness. Guide me, O Holy Spirit, into the spiritual fortress of the presence of God. Amen.

My soul, wait in silence for God only,

For my hope is from Him.

He only is my rock and my salvation,

My stronghold; I shall not be shaken.

Psalm 62.5–6

TWO

THE MOUNTAIN OF GOD

N ow Moses was pasturing the flock of Jethro his father-in-law, the priest of Midian; and he led the flock to the west side of the wilderness and came to Horeb, the mountain of God" (Exod. 3:1).

Mount Horeb was not what it seemed. Though forbidding and barren, Horeb (also called Sinai in Exodus) was the gateway God used to reveal Himself to the Hebrew nation. It was here that the living God appeared in a burning bush to a stammering man named Moses. It was also here that this aged "failure" was sent back to Egypt with miraculous authority to liberate Israel.

It was to Horeb that the Israelites came, following the pillar of fire at night and the covering cloud by day. On Horeb, God Himself inscribed Israel's laws on tablets of stone. Then in the midst of a blazing fire, a deep gloom, and a whirlwind, the terrifying voice of the Most High spoke audibly to His people, thus establishing His covenant with them.

Israel had other sacred places—the tabernacle in the wilderness, the temple in Jerusalem, and various altars men erected to God—but Horeb was unique. Horeb was where Moses and the Israelites met God, and it was where Elijah fled when all he tried had failed.

Horeb was "the mountain of God."

REDEEMER GOD

As a geographic and historic place, Horeb was weighty with spiritual significance. Yet the reality symbolized by Horeb—that God chose a desolate place and then drew desolate men to meet with Him—is a truth that resonates yet today. Horeb's message is this: *the Lord does not turn away from our desolation; He comes to redeem it.*

Consider Moses, the great prince of Egypt. From his high estate, he is exiled for forty years in the wilderness. He marries into a Midianite family and assumes the occupation least esteemed by the Egyptians: a shepherd. Yet it is precisely at Horeb where God meets with Moses and commissions him. It is in a place called "desolation" where Moses finds redemption and returns to Egypt empowered with godlike authority.

> Horeb was weighty with spiritual significance. God chose a desolate place and then drew desolate men to meet with Him. Horeb's message is this: *the Lord does not turn away from our desolation; He comes to redeem it.*

Recall Elijah, the fierce prophet whose spectacular but failed efforts to bring revival burdened him with depression, fear, and discouragement. Elijah also comes to Horeb. The loner, Elijah, who seemingly can't get over the idea that the prophets are dead and he alone is left, discovers that not only are there seven thousand in Israel who are loyal to God, but among them is one, Elisha, who will receive a double portion of Elijah's power. He will bring an end to Jezebel's perverse reign and bring a season of revival to the northern tribes.

On a personal level, Elijah discovers that his true call was not to lead a revival but to "go before" and "prepare the way" for greater things. Indeed it was this very spirit of Elijah that actually prepared the way for Jesus, Israel's Messiah, in the first century, and it shall again be the spirit of Elijah who prepares the way for the second coming of Christ. (See Malachi 4:5–6; Matthew 17:11.)

HOREB IN YOUR WORLD

At Horeb we not only discover more about God but also finally begin to understand ourselves and what the Lord desires of us. Our lives simply and truly focus on that which is most important. Beloved, you know you are at Horeb when God cuts you back to the root source of your spiritual life. Yes, you are at Horeb when you are inwardly repelled by the superficial distractions of modern Christianity and desperate for more of God.

You will not become a better person at Horeb. For Horeb is not about the perfection of self; it's about the abandonment of self. It is about the discovery that in us—in our successes and our failures—there dwells "no good thing." We do not have to perform but conform to the surrendered life of Christ.

> You know you are at Horeb when God cuts you back to the root source of your spiritual life, when you are inwardly repelled by the superficial distractions of modern Christianity and desperate for more of God.

Not everyone who walks with God goes through a Horeb experience. Some find God in worship; others knew desolation prior to knowing Christ and now know only thanksgiving to God for their salvation. Some may have actually been through Horeb but have not identified it as such. At Horeb the morphine of religion wears off, and we can once again feel our pain. Reality manifests. We see ourselves in the light of God, and as we do, we fall upon Christ the cornerstone (Luke 20:18). Though "broken to pieces," we are finally fit to be used by God.

For those who are even now at Horeb, I urge you to let your soul open and your pain rise to God. He knows. He sees your heartache. He feels your sense of shame, bewilderment, and regret. Whatever He says, do it. When you leave Horeb, He will have brought you to a level you previously thought unattainable.

Recall the infusion of life that Moses and Elijah, the men of Horeb, each experienced beyond their season of desolation. Both experienced a type of the resurrection that is to come (Jude; 1 Kings 20). And in a mystery beyond our comprehension, it was these two Horebites who appeared in splendorous glory and spoke with Christ on the Mount of Transfiguration (Matt. 17:1-3).

Horeb, once the place of desolation, is redeemed and revealed as a gateway to God. It is here, in brokenness and fearless honesty, where God brings wholeness of soul.

Horeb is the mountain of God. And once here, we are just steps away from the shelter of the Most High.

> *O living God, I bow before You. I confess my abject need of You. My guard is down, my actor is dead, and with him I fear my dreams are also gone. Yet You give dreams even to old men. You are the Resurrection. I cast myself upon You, O great God of my salvation. Draw me into Your holy shelter, and renew me.*

The LORD also will be a stronghold for the oppressed,

A stronghold in times of trouble;

And those who know Your name will put their trust in You,

For You, O LORD, have not forsaken those who seek You.

—Psalm 9:9–10

THREE

SEEING HIM WHO IS UNSEEN

I T IS ONE thing to be doctrinally familiar with the sacrifice of Jesus Christ, to accept His gift of salvation by faith. It is another thing, however, to actually know Him. For Moses, the experience at Horeb and the unfolding events afterward compelled him not only to serve God but also to be intimately knowledgeable of the Most High.

It was there in the cleft of a rock near Horeb where Moses prayed, "...If I have found favor in Your sight, let me know Your ways that I may know You" (Exod. 33:13).

And in turn, the Lord promised, "My presence shall go with you, and I will give you rest" (v. 14).

We cannot say we truly know God if we remain ignorant of His ways. To know the ways of a person is to know how they would respond to the blessings and challenges of life. While the Lord revealed His *acts* to the sons of Israel, He made known His *ways* to Moses (Ps. 103:7). Moses was familiar with the deeper motives of God's heart; he knew the resolve of the Lord's love and how attracted God was to the lowly.

The Lord promised Moses, "My presence shall go with you..." (Exod. 33:14). When God's presence accompanies our actions, all the energy we once spent worrying and planning is reclaimed and offered back to God in praise and effective service.

The outcome of being companioned through life with Christ is in His next promise: "...I will give you rest" (v. 14). To enter God's rest does not imply that we have become inactive, but that God has become active. Thus Jesus calls, "Come to Me, all who are weary and heavy-laden, and I will give you rest" (Matt. 11:28).

How the church today, weary and desperate, needs to return to Jesus and reenter God's rest! Yoked to Christ, our burdens are transferred to the vastness of His strength and abilities. He becomes to us an untiring resource for our weakness. He is unfailing wisdom for our ignorance. At the place of rest, Christ becomes a continual life spring of grace and virtue. We can cease from our anxious labors and, unfettered from our ideas and traditions, serve Him in the unlimited strength of His might.

> The outcome of being companioned through life with Christ is in His promise: "...I will give you rest." To enter God's rest does not imply that we have become inactive, but that God has become active.

God has always been more concerned with the condition of our hearts than the activity of our hands. What we become *to* Him is far more consequential than all we will ever do *for* Him. He wants our love and companionship. Indeed, the Scriptures tell us, "He jealously desires the Spirit which He has made to dwell in us" (James 4:5). Thus, if our devotion to our task exceeds our devotion to Him, there will be times when He personally hinders our success.

It is out of love that God delivers us from the unanointed momentum of our zeal. He intentionally dries up our vigor. The Lord insists that our success not originate from our strength but from our union with Him. Our time of desolation, brokenness, and disappointment becomes a tool in His hand where He works within us a deeper dependency on His strength.

Alone with God on Horeb, Moses prayed, "...show me Your glory!" (Exod. 33:18).

The Lord responded, "I Myself will make all My goodness pass before you" (v. 19). At the center of Christ's resplendent glory is His incomparable goodness. Indeed, our Horeb experience becomes the very site where, in spite of our sense of failure, God reveals to us His goodness.

THE CAVE OF WITHDRAWAL

Just as God revealed His goodness to Moses, so Elijah, stressed and discouraged, also needed his soul renewed by the goodness of God. It can be a crushing experience to give your very best and still fall short. That is what happened with Elijah. Scripture tells us, "Hope deferred makes the heart sick..." (Prov. 13:12). Elijah became discouraged with his inability to effect revival, and he fled south to Horeb. There he lodged in a cave on the mountainside. He had lost hope that revival would come to Israel.

When we lose hope, we simultaneously lose faith, for faith is the substance of the thing hoped for. Without hope or faith, our lives are desolate and without perspective.

Much of Elijah's discouragement came from the false expectations he had placed on himself. It is human nature to imagine the outcome of our labors. We so easily and prematurely project ourselves into a place of fulfillment. Yet, whatever our task, we must obey God and leave the results of our efforts in His hands.

Elijah withdrew into a cave on Horeb. For us, self-pity can also become a spiritual cave. It can trap us in a dark hole of loneliness and pain. In this place of isolation we fail to hear the encouragement of God. All we really hear is the echo of our own voice magnifying and distorting our problems.

> It is human nature to imagine the outcome of our labors. Yet whatever our task, we must obey God and leave the results of our efforts in His hands.

Elijah was alone and despairing, hiding away in a cave; yet the Lord knew his heart. So the Lord asked him:

> "What are you doing here, Elijah?" He said, "I have been very zealous for the LORD, the God of hosts; for the sons of Israel have forsaken Your covenant, torn down Your altars and killed Your prophets with the sword. And I alone am left; and they seek my life, to take it away."
>
> —1 Kings 19:9–10

Elijah wanted desperately to see the nation awakened, but he did not understand the role God would have him play. Perhaps Elijah's main mistake was that he was personally shouldering the burden of Israel's revival. Not knowing his own place, he assumed the place of God.

Calling Elijah out of the cave, the Lord told him, "Go forth and stand on the mountain before the LORD..." (v. 11). As Elijah stepped out of the cave's darkness, an awesome event occurred.

> And behold, the LORD was passing by! And a great and strong wind was rending the mountains and breaking in pieces the rocks before the LORD; but the LORD was not in the wind. And after the wind an earthquake, but the LORD

was not in the earthquake. And after the earthquake a fire, but the LORD was not in the fire; and after the fire a sound of a gentle blowing.

—1 Kings 19:11–12

A NEW REVELATION OF GOD

There are times when, to lead us on into new authority and blessings, God must liberate us from the container of our previous experiences. The Lord was passing by, but He was not in the wind, the earthquake, or the fire, all of which were familiar symbols to Elijah. The Lord who caused these mighty manifestations was not in them.

For Elijah, mighty manifestations had been signs of God's approval. But something new was at hand that required a fresh submission to the living God. A double portion of power was coming! The distinguishing characteristic of this new anointing would be seen not only in supernatural manifestations, but also in greater wisdom and compassion.

Earthquakes, fires, and storms—the signs that accompanied Elijah—are the signs of our times as well. But the new level God sets before us, the double portion, is more spiritually sophisticated. Thus we must learn to recognize the nearness of the Lord when there are no "earthquakes" or "storms" to capture our attention. He demands we enter a more refined relationship with Him, one that is based on His love and the whisper of His Word, not merely on spiritual phenomena or the issues of our times.

After the last sign, there came "...a gentle blowing" (v. 12). Elijah recognized this holy silence; the thick presence of God was returning. Elijah "…wrapped his face in his mantle…" lest he look upon God (v. 13). Perhaps it was near this very site that Moses, five hundred years earlier, hid when the Lord passed by. Now it was Elijah's turn. Entering this eternal stillness was the person of God.

We too must learn to hear the voice of Him who rarely speaks audibly and observe the actions of Him who is otherwise invisible. Elijah would gain the courage to endure Jezebel's wrath the same way Moses faced the rage of Pharaoh: "…he endured, as seeing Him who is unseen" (Heb. 11:27). We must learn to detect, without great signs, the still, small voice of God.

He will not fight for our attention; He must be sought. He will not startle us; He must be perceived. It took no special skill to "discern" the earthquake, the fire, or the great storm, but to sense the holy quiet of God, our other activities must cease. In our world of great pressures and continual distractions, the attention of our hearts must rise to the invisible world of God's Spirit. We must learn to see Him who is unseen.

As we continue our pursuit for the shelter of the Most High, we will look at the structure and substance of this dwelling of God.

Lord Jesus, I thank You for Your great acts of coming to our world, for Your teaching, healing, and dying for our sins. My heart is full of thanksgiving to You. But, Master, I also desire to know Your ways, that I may know You. Teach me Your ways, O Lord; grant me entrance into Your presence, and, as I enter Your holy shelter, grant rest for my soul.

He who dwells in the shelter of the Most High

Will abide in the shadow of the Almighty.

I will say to the LORD, "My refuge and my fortress,

My God, in whom I trust!"

For it is He who delivers you from the snare of the trapper

And from the deadly pestilence.

He will cover you with His pinions,

And under His wings you may seek refuge;

His faithfulness is a shield and bulwark.

You will not be afraid of the terror by night,

Or of the arrow that flies by day;

Of the pestilence that stalks in darkness,

Or of the destruction that lays waste at noon.

A thousand may fall at your side

And ten thousand at your right hand,

But it shall not approach you.

You will only look on with your eyes

And see the recompense of the wicked.

—Psalm 91:1–8

FOUR

THE STRONGHOLD OF GOD

WHAT MOSES AND Elijah discovered at Horeb is eternally true for us as well: there exists a dwelling place in God's heart where the soul of man can be both sheltered and restored. Let us not doubt, for the words of the ancient hymn are living yet today: our God is indeed a mighty fortress; He is a bulwark never failing.

The dictionary defines *immunity* as "freedom or exemption, as from a penalty, burden, duty, or evil." This is how

35

the living God wants His children to walk, in freedom from the penalties and burdens of sin, delivered from the duties of legalistic religion, protected and triumphant over the assault of the evil one.

Survey the landscape of the Bible. You will find hundreds of examples of God's loving protection. Every time the Lord pleaded with sinful Israel to return to Him, it was to urge them back to His protection; each time they responded, they were secured again within the stronghold of God. The Scriptures say, "…He shielded him and cared for him; he guarded him as the apple of his eye" (Deut. 32:10, NIV).

A FATHER'S CARE

God is not only our Creator, but He is also our Father. As such, it is inconceivable that He would leave His children unprotected. In Matthew 6:8, Jesus says our Father knows our needs before we ask Him. If we, even in our fallen condition, seek to provide for our children, how much more does God in His perfection seek to shelter and care for His offspring!

> The living God wants His children to walk in freedom from the penalties and burdens of sin, delivered from the duties of legalistic religion, protected and triumphant over the assault of the evil one.

Scripture testifies that He has "...granted to us everything pertaining to life and godliness, through the true knowledge of Him who called us by His own glory and excellence" (2 Pet. 1:3). The more we possess a true knowledge of the Almighty, the more accessible His provisions for us become. What has He given us? He has prepared an abiding place for us where everything that we need concerning life and godliness is ours. It is a place where every spiritual blessing in the heavenly places belongs to us in Christ (Eph. 1:3).

David knew of this stronghold. He wrote, "The LORD is my rock and my fortress...in whom I take refuge; My shield and...my stronghold" (Ps. 18:2).

Again, speaking of those who fear God, David prayed, "You hide them in the secret place of Your presence from the conspiracies of man; You keep them secretly in a shelter from the strife of tongues" (Ps. 31:20). And again, "You are my hiding place; You preserve me from trouble; You surround me with songs of deliverance" (Ps. 32:7).

In David's personal life, he knew the living God as a spiritual stronghold and a place of safety from conflict. The king was intimately familiar with this special place in God's presence. It was here in the fortress of God where David's soul was sheltered.

FOR THOSE WHO FOLLOW CHRIST

This stronghold was not just a special provision for prophets and godly kings. From the day of Christ's resurrection, the entrance into the citadel of heaven was opened to all who would follow the Messiah. Discovering this abode where Christ literally floods us with His life is not merely the subject of this book; it is the object of our existence!

How shall we find this spiritual place? We simply begin by loving Jesus. He said, "...he who loves Me will be loved by My Father, and I will love him and will disclose Myself to him" (John 14:21). If we persevere in love and obedience, Jesus has promised to progressively reveal Himself to us.

> If we, even in our fallen condition, seek to provide for our children, how much more does God in His perfection seek to shelter and care for His offspring!

Consider the magnitude of Jesus's promise! He continued, "If anyone loves Me, he will keep My word; and My Father will love him, and We will come to him and make Our abode with him" (John 14:23).

This unfolding revelation of Jesus Christ to our hearts is the path to the abode of God. It is this shelter of the Most High that is the stronghold of God.

In the following chapters, we will enter various dimensions of spiritual protection. We will chart the power that God has for those who are fortressed in His presence. For now, if you have given your life to Christ and are sincere in your desire to

follow Him, it is enough to know that the stronghold of God
awaits you.

> *Lord, with the psalmist I cry, "When shall I enter the*
> *courts of the living God?" You are our Father; do not hide*
> *Yourself from us, Your children! Bring us to Your lap, O*
> *God! Hold us to Your heart; assure us with the fullness of*
> *Your Spirit that You indeed are near. Thank You, Lord!*

For you have made the LORD, my refuge,

Even the Most High, your dwelling place.

No evil will befall you,

Nor will any plague come near your tent.

For He will give His angels charge concerning you,

To guard you in all your ways.

They will bear you up in their hands,

That you do not strike your foot against a stone.

You will tread upon the lion and cobra,

The young lion and the serpent you will trample down.

—Psalm 91:9–13

FIVE

THE WATCHFULNESS OF GOD

THE LORD CONTINUALLY watches our lives. From the moment of our conception to the hour of our death, the Lord guards and guides our earthly journey. The psalmist knew God's watchfulness well. He wrote:

O LORD, You have searched me and known me. You know when I sit down and when I rise up; You understand my thought from afar. You scrutinize my path and my lying down, and are intimately acquainted with all my ways. Even before there is a word on my tongue, Behold, O LORD, You know it all. You have enclosed me behind and before, and laid Your hand upon me.

—Psalm 139:1–5

THE GOD WHO KEEPS US

The Lord sees our unspoken thoughts; before we move He is aware of our motives. He knows everything about us. God has sealed us in the Holy Spirit. From the time we were born again, we were clothed in Christ (Gal. 3:27). We belong to Him. We are His property, bought with the price of His blood. He will not let us go easily.

> A vineyard of wine, sing of it! I, the LORD, am its keeper; I water it every moment. So that no one will damage it, I guard it night and day.
>
> —Isaiah 27:2–3

Even when we do not sense His presence, He is watching and working, guiding us to Himself. It was His working in us that brought us to Himself; it remains His work to renew us in His image. This is His highest priority, and He guards His work "night and day."

Even when we do not sense God's presence, He is watching and working, guiding us to Himself. It was His working in us that brought us to Himself; it remains His work to renew us in His image.

Again the psalmist was resting in his knowledge of God's care when he wrote:

> I will lift up my eyes to the mountains; from where shall my help come? My help comes from the LORD, who made heaven and earth. He will not allow your foot to slip; He who keeps you will not slumber. Behold, He who keeps Israel will neither slumber nor sleep.
>
> —Psalm 121:1–4

According to God's Word, there is a provision made for us that will even keep one's foot from slipping. That provision is the watchfulness of God, where He hedges our path to the shelter He has prepared for us.

GUARDED IN ALL OUR WAYS

The definition of the word *keep* is "to have and retain in one's control or possession." To be kept by God is to be guarded under His control and secured as His possession.

Until we are fully renewed in the spirit of our minds to the point that our minds are absorbed into the mind of Christ

(1 Cor. 2:16; Phil. 2:5), however, our thoughts are not always God's thoughts, nor are our ways always His ways. Thus, Jesus prayed that the Father would keep us from the evil one (John 17:15). In answer to Christ's prayer, the Father has given His angels charge concerning us, to guard us in all our ways (Ps. 91:11; Heb. 1:13–14).

Yet, we have been blind to the presence and work of our angelic friends. We have been like Elisha's servant who was more threatened by his circumstances than he was aware of God's provision:

> Now when the attendant of the man of God had risen early and gone out, behold, an army with horses and chariots was circling the city. And his servant said to him, "Alas, my master! What shall we do?" So he answered, "Do not fear, for those who are with us are more than those who are with them." Then Elisha prayed and said, "O Lord, I pray, open his eyes that he may see." And the Lord opened the servant's eyes and he saw; and behold, the mountain was full of horses and chariots of fire all around Elisha.
>
> —2 Kings 6:15–17

Just as the angels of God surrounded Elisha, so there are angels guarding you. They were at your side protecting you even before you came to Christ.

There may have been a number of times when, had the angels of the Lord not been assigned to you, you might have suffered an untimely death. Indeed there were other times, difficult times, when the Lord's angels strengthened you, carrying you through hardship and tragedy. You wondered, How did I survive? You escaped from Satan's clutches because the Lord assigned His angels to you. They strengthened you in your distress.

There were times when even Jesus needed angelic help. The Scriptures tell us that after the Lord faced severe spiritual warfare in the wilderness, "Then the devil left Him; and behold, angels came and began to minister to Him" (Matt. 4:11). At the end of His life, while sweating blood in fervent prayer, we again read, "Now an angel from heaven appeared to Him, strengthening Him" (Luke 22:43).

> Indeed there were times, difficult times, when the Lord's angels carried you through hardship and tragedy. They strengthened you in your distress.

Wherever Jesus was, the angels of God were always at His side. In His most difficult hour, Jesus reminded Peter of the Father's readiness to provide angelic help. He said, "Or do you think that I cannot appeal to My Father, and He will at once put at My disposal more than twelve legions of angels?" (Matt. 26:53).

God appointed angels to assist and strengthen Jesus, and He has sent angels to assist and strengthen you. As His angels urged Lot and his family to leave Sodom, so angels are urging God's people today to forsake wickedness. Yes, even as you sit and read these words, there are angels watching over you, guarding you as you enter the shelter of the Most High.

Lord Jesus, Your Word tells us that all things are open and laid bare before Your eyes. We also read that Your ears attend to our prayers. Your watchfulness is our comfort and our peace. Yet, Lord, open our eyes as You did the eyes of Elisha's servant, that we might see You. Open our ears that we might hear You. Grant us the peace that comes from knowing Your daily concern for our lives. Amen.

Everyone who comes to Me and hears My words and acts on them, I will show you whom he is like: he is like a man building a house, who dug deep and laid a foundation on the rock; and when a flood occurred, the torrent burst against that house and could not shake it, because it had been well built.

Luke 6:47–48

SIX

GUARDED BY HIS WORD

THE PRIMARY MEANS through which we are kept and preserved by God is through obedience to His Word. In the submission of our will to God, our soul finds protection from evil. Consider the apostle John's words to the young men of the first-century church when he said, "...I have written to you, young men, because you are strong, and the word of God abides in you, and you have overcome the evil one" (1 John 2:14).

Abiding in the Word of God brought spiritual strength

to the young men in John's day, enabling them to overcome the evil one. Is this the reason many of us are defeated by the devil—because we do not abide in the Word?

Christ's teaching guides us into the presence of the Father. It is the Father's presence that both empowers and protects us. Jesus said:

> My sheep hear My voice, and I know them, and they follow Me; and I give eternal life to them, and they will never perish; and no one will snatch them out of My hand. My Father, who has given them to Me, is greater than all; and no one is able to snatch them out of the Father's hand.
> —John 10:27–29

No one is stronger than our heavenly Father. As we follow Christ, He positions us in the palm of God's hand. There death cannot seize us. Whatever battles we face, we never face them alone. There is none like our God. "The eternal God is a dwelling place, and underneath are the everlasting arms; and He drove out the enemy from before you, and said, 'Destroy!'" (Deut. 33:27).

Underneath our every step are God's everlasting arms. Thus, when we pass through spiritual conflicts and trials, we are walking on eternal ground, continually kept by the power of Christ's indestructible life (Heb. 7:16). Even when we pass through the shadow of death itself, the powers of death cannot hold us. They are kept at bay by His command.

> For I am convinced that neither death, nor life, nor angels, nor principalities, nor things present, nor things to come, nor powers, nor height, nor depth, nor any other created

thing, will be able to separate us from the love of God, which is in Christ Jesus our Lord.

—Romans 8:38–39

THOSE WHO NEVER SEE DEATH

The Spirit of God is forever redeeming and transforming all that we encounter, causing each event to work for our spiritual good. Indeed it has been truly stated that rescue is the constant pattern of God's activity. His final act of encouragement is the Resurrection.

> Underneath our every step are God's everlasting arms. Thus when we pass through spiritual conflicts and trials, we are walking on eternal ground, continually kept by the power of Christ's indestructible life.

Jesus promised, "Truly, truly, I say to you, if anyone keeps My word he will never see death" (John 8:51). The Jews to whom Jesus spoke were offended by this statement. They lacked divine logic and the view of life from eternity. They were ignorant of the resurrection power given every follower of Christ.

Before we judge them too harshly, however, let us ask ourselves, "Are we offended by Christ's promise?" Given the fact that everyone who followed Jesus in the first century died, are we ashamed of the apparent contradictions of this promise? Do we really believe we will never see death?

The Jews also were perplexed. They countered, saying, "Now we know that You have a demon. Abraham died, and the prophets also; and You say, 'If anyone keeps My word, he shall never taste of death'" (John 8:52). But Jesus did not say that His followers would never taste death. He said we would never see death.

Certainly there are times when we seem engulfed by sorrow, trapped in an incubator of death itself. Yet, this is a glory of our faith: though we die, we do not see death; we see life. We will taste death, but as Christians, we ingest life.

> Jesus promised, "If anyone keeps My word he will never see death." Are we offended by Christ's promise? Do we really believe we will never see death?

Yes, if we keep Christ's Word throughout the trial, His promise to us is that we will "never see death." For those who live by every word that comes from the mouth of God, the final outcome of each struggle is not death but life in abundance. Jesus said:

> But you will be betrayed even by parents and brothers and relatives and friends, and they will put some of you to death, and you will be hated by all because of My name. Yet not a hair of your head will perish.
>
> —Luke 21:16–18

He said we may be put to death, yet not even a hair on our heads will perish. Is not death the cessation of life? If death is due to illness, is it not the progressive diminishing of life?

Yet, in Christ, every darkened, shadowy valley into which our human experience descends is predestined to surface in a broad field of life. We taste death but do not see it.

David said, "Even though I walk through the valley of the shadow of death, I fear no evil, for You are with me..." (Ps. 23:4). As frightening as death seems, for those who keep the Word of the Lord, death is no more a barrier than a shadow. For what dies in us is that which was foreordained to die—the husk of our old nature. While the death of self is a daily choice, our new inner nature does not die.

"Therefore we do not lose heart, but though our outer man is decaying, yet our inner man is being renewed day by day" (2 Cor. 4:16). Yes, in the experience of our own hearts we have the demonstration of God's resurrection power, effectual both now and in the future. As we keep Christ's Word, our difficulties always culminate in eternal life. We join Paul in thanking God, "Who always leads us in triumph in Christ, and manifests through us the sweet aroma of the knowledge of Him in every place" (2 Cor. 2:14).

In the many faces of death, in spite of our failures, sicknesses, and difficulties, there remains a stronghold. It is here in our holding fast the Word of life that the Lord "...keeps [us], and the evil one does not touch [us]" (1 John 5:18).

There will be a time when, from the vantage point of heaven, we will review our life's experiences. In glorious retrospect we shall see every occasion when destruction stood against us. And we will also see that it was here, in these very difficulties, that Christ revealed within us His resurrection power! Though we walked through the valley of the shadow of death, we did not die. Rather, we learned to fear no evil. From heaven's view, with awe we will one day say, "Truly, I have never seen death."

Lord, it is true. Even now, I know that You have been with me in every trial and battle. Because of Your redemptive power, I have become stronger in the very conflicts through which Satan meant to weaken me; I have prospered in the very battles through which the devil sought to destroy me!

Truly, You have worked all things for good in my life. And even in the areas where I have yet to understand Your purposes, I entrust those also to You. For I know that because of Your grace, even what seems to be the finality of death itself shall be transformed; and in all things I shall know only the power of Your resurrection life. Amen.

For the LORD's portion is His people;

Jacob is the allotment of His inheritance.

He found him in a desert land,

And in the howling waste of a wilderness;

He encircled him, He cared for him,

He guarded him as the pupil of His eye.

Like an eagle that stirs up its nest,

That hovers over its young,

He spread His wings and caught them,

He carried them on His pinions.

—Deuteronomy 32:9–11

SEVEN

THE TRANSFORMED HEART

THE LORD HAS not promised us a world without hardship, but that, in the midst of hardship, He will be revealed through us.

CHRIST: THE GREAT I AM

What is God's primary purpose for us? Why were we created? From the beginning of time, God created man with one purpose: to make us in His image according to His likeness.

The Lord has never changed His divine intent toward

us. Indeed, Paul tells us that God causes all things in our lives to work toward the good of this one eternal goal (Rom. 8:28–29).

What of the difficulties and tribulations that we encounter in this life? In the scheme of God's plan, troubles and afflictions are upgraded to classroom lessons where we learn to appropriate the nature of Christ. Thus our difficulties compel us toward God, and He compels us toward Christlikeness and change. And the Lord speaks to each of us His promise:

> Fear not, for I have redeemed you; I have summoned you by name; you are mine. When you pass through the waters, I will be with you; and when you pass through the rivers, they will not sweep over you. When you walk through the fire, you will not be burned; the flames will not set you ablaze. For I am the LORD, your God, the Holy One of Israel, your Savior.
>
> —Isaiah 43:1–3, NIV

While His pledge is a great encouragement, we should be mindful that the Lord did not say He would keep us from the fire or the floodwaters, but He would be with us in them.

Jesus still manifests Himself in the storms of our times, defying what seem to be impossible conditions in order to reach us. He is the master of every human distress; He can help us in every circumstance.

Why does the Lord allow us to pass through conflict in the first place? Because it is here that He trains His sons and daughters in Christlikeness.

Recall the story of Jesus's disciples when they were without Him on a turbulent sea (Matt. 14:22–33). Their boat had been battered by the heaving waves and contrary wind. Jesus, walking on the water, came to them sometime in the early morning. His first words were those of comfort when He said, "Take courage, it is I; do not be afraid" (Matt. 14:27).

THE FATHER'S HIGHEST PURPOSE

It is important to note that the words Christ uses in His assurance, "It is I," is translated other places within Scripture as: "I AM." This phrase is the divine appellation—the eternal designation of God. While Jesus indeed comes to the aid of His disciples, He also reveals Himself transcendent of time's barriers. As such, He proclaims His availability to all His disciples. He is God with us, even to the end of the age!

Thus, Jesus still comes to His disciples' aid, manifesting Himself in the storms of our times, defying what seem to be impossible conditions in order to reach us. He is the master of every human distress; He can help us in every circumstance.

Let us silence the fretting unbelief of our hearts. Christ is capable, even at this moment, to reach us. Look through the storm until you sense His presence, until you hear His confident voice saying, "Take courage; it is I."

Yet, Jesus has more on His mind than comforting His disciples. It is one thing to trust Christ to calm the storm around us; it is another matter to leave our security and venture out with Him on the water! This very setting of raging wind and sea is the classroom that the Son of God seeks to perfect His disciples' faith.

Let us affirm the Father's highest purpose for us: Jesus did not come simply to console us but to perfect us! This is exactly where He will take us once we are willing. To behold Christ's goal of perfection for us is to truly gaze into another dimension of God.

We should repent of carrying the image of a Savior who fails to confront our sin or challenge our unbelief, for such is a false image of God. If we are to genuinely know Him, we must accept this truth: Jesus Christ is irrevocably committed to our complete transformation!

COMPELLED TOWARD GOD

Of all the disciples, Peter alone responds to the occasion with vision and faith. Putting his hands on the upper plank of the rolling boat's side, Peter peers through the dark night and windblown spray and calls to Jesus, saying, "Lord, if it is You, command me to come to You on the water" (Matt. 14:28). There is faith in Peter's voice!

Jesus summons His disciple, "Come!"

Peter swings his legs over the edge, dangling them above the swirling sea. With his eyes fixed on Jesus, he steps out, letting his full weight follow both the downward movement of his feet and the upward reach of his faith.

Incredibly, Peter is now standing and walking on the rolling waves toward Jesus!

In the purest sense, however, Peter did not rest his weight on the water; he stood on Christ's word: "Come!" Peter trusted that if Jesus told him to do the impossible—even to walk on the water—the power to obey would be inherent within the command.

Moments later Peter's faith faltered. He began to sink. But there is something extraordinary to be seen in Christ's response—a view into Christ's actual nature and His ultimate purpose. Jesus did not commend or congratulate Peter. He rebuked him! We would have expected praise and encouragement, but none came.

Was Jesus angry? No. The truth is, Jesus Christ is relentlessly given to our perfection. He knows that wherever we settle spiritually will be far short of His provision. He also knows that the more we are transformed into His image, the less vulnerable we are to the evils of this world. Thus He compels us toward difficulties, for they compel us toward God, and God compels us toward change. And it is the transformed heart that finds the shelter of the Most High.

> Jesus Christ is relentlessly given to our perfection. He knows that wherever we settle spiritually will be far short of His provision. He also knows that the more we are transformed into His image, the less vulnerable we are to the evils of this world.

Lord Jesus, forgive me for fearing during the storms of life. For too long I have not understood Your commitment to my perfection. I have wanted to be saved without being transformed. I have feared the fullness of becoming Christlike.

Bring forth in me Your faith. Help me to not misinterpret Your encouragement toward excellence when I fall short. With all my heart, I want to glorify You with my life. Grant me the grace that, when others see what You have accomplished in me, they too will glorify You! Amen.

For the LORD gives wisdom;

From His mouth come knowledge and understanding.

He stores up sound wisdom for the upright;

He is a shield to those who walk in integrity,

Guarding the paths of justice,

And He preserves the way of His godly ones.

Then you will discern righteousness and justice

And equity and every good course.

For wisdom will enter your heart

And knowledge will be pleasant to your soul;

Discretion will guard you,

Understanding will watch over you,

To deliver you from the way of evil.

—Proverbs 2:6–12

EIGHT

GREATER PURITY, GREATER PROTECTION

WHEN WE ARE young in Christ, God accepts us as babes. There comes a time, however, when He begins to deal with us as sons.

No Shelter for Evil

There are certain aspects of our lives that exist outside of divine protection, and God Himself seeks to destroy them. We must realize that our carnal nature will find no permanent shelter within God's stronghold, nor will demonic strongholds of deceit, fear, or lust find divine protection.

To find the shelter of God, we must stand with the Lord against sin and compromise. These things must be destroyed or they will destroy us. The transformation of our souls positions us outside the devil's reach. It raises us up spiritually to seat us in heavenly places.

It is one thing to know doctrinally that we are positioned with Christ in heaven; it is quite another thing to spiritually function in that lofty place. (See Ephesians 1:20; 2:6.) To motivate us toward Christlikeness, the Holy Spirit not only instructs us in doctrinal truths, but He also thrusts us into storms of conflict and satanic assault. It is in the midst of this confrontation with hell that He works in us the virtues of heaven.

LED BY THE SPIRIT

Our walk with God progresses from learning lessons to having what we just learned tested. This was the Father's pattern with His Son, and it is His pattern with us as well. Let us, therefore, consider Jesus.

Just after Christ was baptized by John, the Father affirmed His sonship. What was the next scene? Jesus was compelled by the Holy Spirit into the wilderness.

When we think about being "Spirit led," we envision miracles, healings, and winning the multitudes. But before Jesus was led to do wonders, He was led to do battle; and the war was over the purity of His heart. Jesus was "led up by the Spirit...to be tempted by the devil" (Matt. 4:1). As much as the Father loved

His Son, as perfectly as He knew Him, yet still the Father proved the character of His Son through conflict.

The word *tempted* actually means "tested or proven in adversity." Jesus was always without sin, yet He learned obedience through the things He suffered. Likewise, the Father is not hesitant about allowing the enemy a measured assault against us. He is not worried that we will break. In fact, He desires a certain degree of brokenness before He can use us.

> To find the shelter of God, we must stand with the Lord against sin and compromise. These things must be destroyed or they will destroy us.

It is in spiritual warfare that what God has taught us is proven. How do you pass the tests of God? There is one answer, one result that guarantees our triumph: to become like Jesus in the midst of our test.

Life consists of learning lessons and passing tests. The integrity of God requires that our learning not be mere head knowledge but that our hearts be conformed to Christ. Indeed, before the Lord is through with us, the way of Christ will be more than something we know; it will be something we instinctively choose in the midst of temptation or battle. This is where we graduate into the power of God.

Entering the shelter of the Most High is the result of a lasting work of God in our lives. Jesus compared the extent of yielded-ness in His disciples' hearts to a man who "…dug deep and laid a foundation on the rock…" (Luke 6:48). It is good that He topples our old nature and tests our newest virtues. For, ultimately, the work that God effects, protects.

> Before the Lord is through with us, the way of Christ will be more than something we know; it will be something we instinctively choose in the midst of temptation or battle. This is where we graduate into the power of God.

Let the storms come. Do not fear the threat of life's fire. God has promised to be with us in our adversity. It is there we attain greater purity, and in greater purity is found greater protection.

Lord Jesus, You said that the pure in heart will see God. Purify me, O Lord. Cleanse me of double-mindedness. Deliver me from selfishness and pride.

Lord, I know that in Your earthly life You only did those things You saw the Father do. Create in me those restraints that crucify my instinctive reactions; release me from the captivity of self-preservation. Deliver me from all pursuits except following You. Establish deep in my life the fire of Your glory. Amen.

As for you also, because of the blood of My covenant with you, I have set your prisoners free from the waterless pit. Return to the stronghold, O prisoners who have the hope; this very day I am declaring that I will restore double to you.

—Zechariah 9:11–12

NINE

The Blood Covenant

THE CONCEPT OF uniting with another person in a lifelong covenant is unfamiliar in this world where contractual agreements are readily nullified and divorce is rampant. Because we are not acquainted with the ramifications of making and keeping a covenant, we fail to utilize the eternal power that is already ours through our covenant relationship with God.

From ancient times, a covenant was the highest form of mutual commitment and unity that any two individuals could express. In the Bible, the word *covenant* means to "fetter together." A covenant bound you for life to your covenant partner. It signified that two people had become one.

Often the participants would pass a sword between themselves to represent that any enemy who attacked one party would find both parties set against him. It was a way of saying, "My arms will be as your arms. My weapons will be as your weapons."

Another ceremony that accompanied the making of a covenant consisted of passing a sandal from one to another. This act symbolized each individual's commitment to travel as far as would be needed to stand with his friend.

Still another ritual called for the two individuals to sacrifice an animal to God; after splitting the sacrifice, each then walked between the halves. From that time on, each covenant partner would consider himself half of the "new person"—born of their oath.

Because the covenant was a lifelong pledge and often included one's descendants, it was not made quickly or without formality. Indeed, it was the highest expression of mutual commitment. Whether the covenant union was consummated between friends, a husband and wife, or between God and man, there was no greater expression of one's commitment to another. The covenant was the deepest, most enduring commitment between two souls.

History of Covenants in the Bible

The Bible is specifically divided along covenant lines. What we call the Old and New Testaments should be translated Old and

New Covenants. The Scriptures reveal that, at various times in history, the Lord initiated covenants with His servants. Of these there were seven major covenants, six of which God made with the following Old Testament partners: Noah, Abraham, Isaac, Jacob, Moses, and David. The seventh and greatest covenant came in the New Testament between the Father and His Son.

> It was not the ark that protected Noah; it was the covenant he had with God. The covenant supplied everything. When one is in covenant with God, he can cease striving; he can rest from the struggle concerning God's plan for his life.

To further understand the nature of God and His covenant relationships with man, let us look at some examples of God's covenants in the Scriptures. In Genesis 6:5, we read that the world had become exceedingly wicked; but one man, Noah, found favor with God. This man became God's partner in a covenant that preserved the human race. The Lord told Noah, "But I will establish My covenant with you; and you shall enter the ark—you and your sons and your wife, and your sons' wives with you" (Gen. 6:18).

When the Lord begins to move in covenant power, His partner is but one component in a series of divine initiatives orchestrated by God. Consider Noah: Even before he was preserved through the flood, the Lord had preserved his righteousness in spite of the violence and perversion around him. God then called Noah and commissioned him to build the ark. Noah did not have to invent the ark; God gave him the plans. Noah did not search out and bring in the animals—God brought them in. And after they entered the ark, Scripture says the Lord closed the door behind them.

It was not the ark that protected Noah; it was the covenant he had with God. The covenant supplied everything Noah and his family needed to survive the world's greatest calamity. Indeed Noah's name means "rest." Noah never questioned if there would really be a flood or how to build an ark. Noah did not waver in unbelief, wondering whether the entire venture was his idea or God's. When one is in covenant with God, he can cease striving; he can rest from the struggle concerning God's plan for his life.

Such is the power supplied to man through a covenant with God. Again, the covenant provides more than what good people can accomplish by trying to be good. It releases more than what clever church people can attain by their own resourcefulness.

Beyond holding to the faith that God Himself inspired, the success of the covenant purpose does not depend on man. Indeed, the final goal of the covenant is to provide a sweeping display of divine power that ultimately and perfectly brings glory to God. Thus the promise of God to Noah—"I will establish My covenant with you"—is itself the assurance that what God has promised will certainly come to pass.

ABRAHAM'S COVENANT

Consider Abraham. The God of glory appeared to Abraham while he was still in Mesopotamia. God called and prepared His servant, who was originally named Abram (exalted father), promising him that he would become the heir of the world and "the father of a multitude of nations" (Abraham). (See Genesis 17.)

Abraham believed God, leaving the land of his forefathers to sojourn in Canaan as an alien. But a time came when the Lord again appeared to His servant. God said, "...Do not fear, Abram, I am a shield to you; your reward shall be very great" (Gen. 15:1).

Abraham engaged in a faith dialogue with God: "Abram said, 'O Lord God, what will You give me, since I am childless...'" (v. 2). God's servant was not expressing doubt, but he was seeking to fulfill his faith.

The Lord responded, "Now look toward the heavens, and count the stars, if you are able to count them....So shall your descendants be" (v. 5). The next verse reads, "Then he believed in the Lord; and He reckoned it to him as righteousness" (v. 6).

There is a more consequential level of faith available to us, one that goes beyond believing that someday God is going to do something important with our lives. It is a faith that realizes God is calling us to significance now. This is the type of faith the Lord awakened in Abraham. That night the Creator Himself covenanted with Abraham. God told His servant to bring a heifer, a goat, a ram, a turtledove, and a young pigeon. "Then he brought all these to Him and cut them in two, and laid each half opposite the other..." (v. 10).

At this point the Lord told Abraham that the Israelites would be strangers enslaved in a strange land for four hundred years but that they would return to the land God had promised him.

> It came about when the sun had set, that it was very dark, and behold, there appeared a smoking oven and a flaming torch which passed between these pieces. On that day the LORD made a covenant with Abram, saying, "To your descendants I have given this land."
>
> —Genesis 15:17–18

Perhaps the smoking oven and flaming torch were prophetic types of when God would lead Israel back to this land, sheltered under a cloud by day and guided by a fire at night. It is also significant that in a typical covenant agreement, both parties would walk between the halves of the sacrifice. Yet in this instance, only the flaming torch passed between the sacrificed animals, suggesting that the Lord would keep both His commitment and Abraham's!

THE COVENANT THROUGH OBEDIENCE

When a covenant was initiated by God, it contained the Lord's unalterable commitment to supply grace and faith to His human counterpart. Again, we see that the initiative for the covenant came from God. Abraham's faith went from "doctrinal" knowledge of God's purposes to a living response.

The Lord also covenanted with Moses on Mount Sinai (also called Horeb). This covenant, however, was not an unequivocal guarantee of divine support. It was a pledge based on national obedience to God's laws, the Ten Commandments. The Lord's support and empowerment of Israel were conditional, not automatic; they were based on Israel's obedience.

They put the commandments into a gold-lined chest called the ark of the covenant. When Israel went to war, they did so with the ark of the covenant before them. The covenant was the power source of their armies; God Himself was their ally in battles. When they crossed the Jordan on their return to Canaan, the ark of the covenant rested on the shoulders of the priests; it caused the waters to part so that the entire nation could possess their inheritance. The power of Israel was in its covenant with God.

THE NEW COVENANT

The entire covenant process is something initiated, established, confirmed, and fulfilled by an act of divine will. The response of God's covenant partner is simply to believe in the integrity of God's promise and obey the covenant conditions.

As Christians, we are a covenant people. The power of redemption in what we describe as the "Christian life" is power springing from an eternal covenant. Our relationship with God is a covenant relationship through Christ. He is the author and perfecter. He is the source, the guide, and the goal of our entire salvation process.

So, we see that God is a covenant-making, covenant-keeping God. And, of course, the greatest covenant that was ever initiated, fulfilling all other covenants, is the covenant relationship between the Father and the Son: the blood covenant.

The terms of this covenant were profound. If the Son of God would live in perfect sinlessness throughout His life, if He then presented His unblemished life to God in redemptive surrender, from that moment into all eternity God would pardon every soul seeking forgiveness. The Father promised in His covenant agreement with His Son to transfer all of mankind's sins onto the cross of Christ.

Today we are forgiven not for any other reason but because Jesus kept the covenant conditions. We have access to God and forgiveness of sins through Jesus. Every time Satan seeks to condemn us for our sins or accuse us of our failures, we have only to remember the blood of Christ. Our salvation was never based on our goodness or our works. The foundation of our faith rests on what Jesus Christ won for us in His covenant with God the Father.

Let us also recognize and rejoice: God did not covenant with a mere man—one limited in vision and weak in fulfillment. In the New Covenant, God covenanted with God. In Christ, we are children of God. As such, we are "...heirs also, heirs of God and fellow heirs with Christ" (Rom. 8:17). Just as Noah's family reaped the protection of God through Noah's covenant, so we receive access into the shelter of the Most High God through Christ. And as Abraham's descendants enjoyed God's covenant promises with Abraham, so we inherit the blessings of all God's covenant promises made to Jesus.

Every time we see a rainbow in the sky, we are reminded that the Lord is a covenant-keeping God. Each remembrance of Israel, once scattered but now returned to the very land promised by God to Abraham, tells us the Almighty is faithful to His covenant promises.

Because of Jesus, God has revealed His willingness to come from as far as eternity to be at our side. God's divine commitment—His *covenant* commitment—is given to us. God united with His covenant partners—you and me—against evil.

Our enemies of sickness, poverty, and fear are His enemies. His enemies of sin and Satan are our adversaries as well. The sword has been passed between us; we stand back to back with God against our common foes.

> Every time Satan seeks to condemn us for our sins or accuse us of our failures, we have only to remember the blood of Christ. Our salvation was never based on our goodness or our works. The foundation of our faith rests on what Jesus Christ won for us in His covenant with God the Father.

The covenant animal of sacrifice is not a bull or a goat; it is a lamb. God and man pass through the "halves" of Christ. We unite with God through Christ's humanity; God unites with us through Christ's divinity. In Jesus, God and man become one in covenant power.

> *How awesome You are, Lord. You gave Your life in covenant with God for me. I know no love like Yours, no goodness comparable to You. There is none like You; no, not one. Grant me the courage to live in a covenant relationship with You. Grant me the faith that knows You are on my side against sickness and fear and that I am on Your side against sin and evil. In the power of Your covenant, I shall know complete victory.*

May Christ through your faith [actually] dwell (settle down, abide, make His permanent home) in your hearts! May you be rooted deep in love and founded securely on love, that you may have the power and be strong to apprehend and grasp with all the saints [God's devoted people, the experience of that love] what is the breadth and length and height and depth [of it]; [that you may really come] to know [practically, through experience for yourselves] the love of Christ, which far surpasses mere knowledge [without experience]; that you may be filled [through all your being] unto all the fullness of God [may have the richest measure of the divine Presence, and become a body wholly filled and flooded with God Himself]!

—Ephesians 3:17–19, AMP

TEN

The Baptism of Love

IT IS HARD for us in this anxious, fearful age to quict our souls and actually dwell upon God in our hearts. We can engage ourselves with Bible study or other acts of obedience. In varying degrees we know how to witness, exhort, and bless. We know how to analyze these things and even perfect them. But to lift our souls above the material world and consciously ponder on God Himself seems beyond the reach of our Christian experience.

TO DWELL UPON GOD

Yet, to actually grasp the substance of God is to enter a spiritual place of immunity; it is to receive into our spirits the victory Christ won for us, which is oneness with God in Christ.

Thus we cannot content ourselves merely with the tasks we are called to perform. Ultimately we will discover that study and church attendance are but forms that have little satisfaction in and of themselves. These activities must become what the Lord has ordained them to be: means through which we seek and find God. Our pleasure will be found not in the mechanics of spiritual disciplines, but in that these disciplines bring us closer to God.

Paul's cry was, "That I may know Him..." (Phil. 3:10). It was this desire to know Jesus that produced Paul's knowledge of salvation, church order, evangelism, and End Time events. Out of his heart's passion to know God came revelation, the writing of Scriptures, and knowledge of the eternal.

Paul's knowledge was based on his experience with Christ.

On the other hand, we have contented ourselves not with seeking the face of God, but with studying the facts of God. We are satisfied with a religion about Christ, without the reality of Christ.

The Bible is the historical record of man's experiences with the Almighty. Out of the personal encounters that people had with the living God, our theological perspectives have developed. But knowledge about God is only the first step toward entering the presence of God. As much as the Bible is a book of truths, it is also a map to God. As Christians, we study and debate the map yet too often fail to make the journey.

LOVE SURPASSES KNOWLEDGE

There is a place greater than knowledge; it is a simple yet eternally profound place where we actually abide in Christ's love. This is, indeed, the shelter of the Most High. Remember the apostle's prayer was that we each would "know the love of Christ which surpasses knowledge..." (Eph. 3:19). As important as knowledge is, that verse tells us love "surpasses knowledge." Doctrinal knowledge is the framework, the vehicle, that opens the door toward divine realities, but love causes us to be "...filled up to all the fullness of God" (v. 19).

> As much as the Bible is a book of truths, it is also a map to God. As Christians, we study and debate the map yet too often fail to make the journey.

There is a dwelling place of love that God desires us to enter. It is a place where our knowledge of God is fulfilled with the substance of God. The Amplified Bible's rendering states:

> May Christ through your faith [actually] dwell (settle down, abide, make His permanent home) in your hearts! May you be rooted deep in love and founded securely on love, that you may have the power and be strong to apprehend and grasp with all the saints [God's devoted people, the experience of that love] what is the breadth and length and height and depth [of it]; [that you may really come]

to know [practically, through experience for yourselves] the love of Christ, which far surpasses mere knowledge [without experience]; that you may be filled [through all your being] unto all the fullness of God [may have the richest measure of the divine Presence, and become a body wholly filled and flooded with God Himself]!

—Ephesians 3:17–19

Is this not our goal to be rooted deeply in love; to grasp the breadth, length, height, and depth of God's love; and to know for ourselves the deep, personal love of Christ? Can any goal be more wonderful? Indeed to be filled and flooded with God Himself is the very hope of the gospel!

> There is a dwelling place of love that God desires us to enter. It is a place where our knowledge of God is fulfilled with the substance of God.

You see, God cannot truly be known without in some way also being experienced. If you had never seen a sunrise or a starry night sky, could any description substitute for your own eyes beholding the expansive beauty? Awe comes from seeing and encountering, not merely from knowing that somewhere a beautiful sky exists.

Likewise, to truly know God we must seek Him until we pass through the outer, informational realm about God and actually find for ourselves the living presence of the Lord Himself.

This is the "upward call" of God in Christ Jesus. It draws us through our doctrines into the immediacy of the divine presence. The journey leaves us in the place of transcendent surrender where we listen to His voice and, from listening, ascend into His love.

The earth's last great move of God shall be distinguished by an outpouring from Christ of irresistible desire for His people. To those who truly yearn for His appearing, there shall come, in ever-increasing waves, seasons of renewal from the presence of the Lord. (See Acts 3:19–21.) Intimacy with Christ shall be restored to its highest level since the first century.

Many on the outside of this move of God as well as those touched and healed by it will look and marvel: "How did these common people obtain such power?" They will see miracles similar to when Jesus Christ walked the earth. Multitudes will be drawn into the valley of decision. For them, the kingdom of God will truly be at hand.

But for those whom the Lord has drawn to Himself, there will be no mystery as to how He empowered them. Having returned to the simplicity and purity of devotion to Christ, they will have received the baptism of love.

> *Is this possible, my Lord? Is it true that I might know the love of God that surpasses all knowledge? O God, I seek to know You, to live in the substance of Your love.*

For Your love is the shelter of my protection. Help me, Master, to recognize Your love, not as a divine emotion, but as Your very substance! Help me to see that it was neither Pilate nor Satan that put You on the cross; it was love alone to which You succumbed. Remind me again that it is Your love that still intercedes for me even now.

...The LORD is my rock and my fortress and my deliverer;

My God, my rock, in whom I take refuge,

My shield and the horn of my salvation, my stronghold and my

refuge;

My savior, You save me from violence.

I call upon the LORD, who is worthy to be praised,

And I am saved from my enemies.

—2 Samuel 22:2–4

ELEVEN

WHERE EVERY PRAYER IS ANSWERED

W E SHOULD NOT assume that simply because we are Christians we have learned the secret of abiding in Christ. Jesus said, "If you abide in Me, and My words abide in you, ask whatever you wish, and it will be done for you" (John 15:7). To abide in Him is to live in ceaseless fusion with His passions. It is to have found the habitation of God where no barrier or shadow exists between our weakness and His sufficiency, or between our yearning and His fulfillment.

93

Considering the size of God's promises, it is actually a misfortune that most of us have no more than a few minutes of devotions each day and a church service or two each week.

The shelter of God is not only a place to visit God, but it is also a place to dwell with Him. For those who dwell with God, His presence is not merely our refuge; it is a permanent address. When we are abiding in Christ, even as He and the Father are One, so we become one with Him. It is His life, His virtue, His wisdom, and His Spirit that sustain us. We become perfectly weak, unable to resist Him. Like the Son's relationship with the Father, so we do nothing from our own initiative unless it is something we see Him do. If He should require of us nothing more than our love, we are well content. Jesus is our first choice, not our last resort.

> To abide in Christ is to have found the habitation of God where no barrier or shadow exists between our weakness and His sufficiency, or between our yearning and His fulfillment.

To those who have entered the abiding place, our questions are not about doctrines or pronouncing the right prayer at an altar. We have found Him whom our soul loves. We are constrained and guided by His voice, surrendered and imprisoned in His love. He says, "O my dove, in the clefts of the rock, in the secret place of the steep pathway, let me see your form, let me hear your voice; for your voice is sweet, and your form is lovely" (Song of Sol. 2:14).

This communion of heart between Christ and His bride is a stronghold. It is God's shelter from the distresses and distractions of life. Here He tells us what to pray; here our supplications are answered. Yet in spite of our flaws and the weakness of our prayers, to Him our voice is sweet; in spite of our lowliness, our form is lovely in His eyes.

IN THE BOSOM OF CHRIST

What are we to Jesus? Has He given us life only to test His creative skills? No. We exist for the fulfillment of His love. "…As He had loved those who were His own in the world, He loved them to the last and to the highest degree" (John 13:1, AMP).

You are loved by the Lord. He appreciates you. Jesus personally died for each of us; He prays to the Father for us by name. You say, "But I am full of fears, wrought with failure."

He says, "Father, I want them with me—these you've given me—so that they can see my glory" (John 17:24, TLB).

Christ appreciates us because we are a gift to Him from the Father. Jesus knows that the Father gives only good gifts (James 1:17). Yes, we are imperfect, but Christ sees us in our ultimate completeness. Seeing the end from the beginning, He joyfully receives us.

And what kind of gift are we? Are we a reward, or perhaps a challenge? No. We are His bride. The glance of our eyes makes

His heart beat faster (Song of Sol. 4:9). And it is here, in the love we share with Jesus, that we are secured in God's shelter.

Yes, we are imperfect, but Christ sees us in our ultimate completeness. Seeing the end from the beginning, He joyfully receives us. We are His bride.

Lord, forgive me for the inconsistency of my commitment to You. Lord, I abandon any dwelling place of self. Grant me Your power that I might truly abide in You; grant me obedience that I might sustain Your abiding Word in me. With all that I am, I desire unbroken fellowship with You. Even now, shape me to fit perfectly into Your presence, that I might dwell in oneness with You, that I might live empowered by the impulse of Your will.

Because he has loved Me, therefore I will deliver him;
I will set him securely on high, because he has known
My name.
He will call upon Me, and I will answer him;
I will be with him in trouble;
I will rescue him and honor him.
With a long life I will satisfy him
And let him see My salvation.

—Psalm 91:14–16

TWELVE

The Power of His Name

WITH WHAT EARNESTNESS we have read Christ's words: "Whatever you ask in My name, that will I do, so that the Father may be glorified in the Son" (John 14:13). How is it that this promise is not fulfilled for us? Why is it that such great anticipation results in such a small return?

Think of the implications if Jesus's words are actually true! Any sickness can be healed; any demon can be cast out. Any sinner, friend, or relative can be saved. He said,

"Whatever you ask…" Who is to stop our faith from reaching even a greater fulfillment? Not only can any person be healed, but also any city; not merely can any demon be cast out, but also any principality can be brought down. The ends of the earth await the awakening of our faith to Christ's promise!

Yet, like the rich young ruler, we know something is missing in us. We ask the Master, "What still do we lack?" In the Gospel of John, chapter 14, Jesus continues, "If you ask Me anything in My name, I will do it. If you love Me, you will keep My commandments" (vv. 14–15). Jesus will not spontaneously answer our requests until we instinctively obey Him. Obedience to His requests prepares us to experience His indwelling, where His love finds its fulfillment.

> Not only can any person be healed, but also any city; not merely can any demon be cast out, but also any principality can be brought down. The ends of the earth await the awakening of our faith to Christ's promise!

It is vital that we obey Him, but Christ's ultimate goal is not only our obedience, but also our oneness with Him. He would rather dwell intimately in just one of His servants' hearts than to have ten thousand who know Him from afar. He is after our love. And what is love? It is a passion for oneness.

"He who has My commandments and keeps them is the one who loves Me; and he who loves Me will be loved by My Father, and I will love him and will disclose Myself to him" (v. 21). Obedience born of love leads to greater love; greater love ultimately leads to the open disclosure of Christ to our hearts.

"I will love him and will disclose Myself to him." Let us read these words over and over again. Let us arouse our spirits to the deep, holy desire that dwells not only in Christ's promise but also in His heart. Jesus longed for continued fellowship with His disciples. Thus He was preparing them for intimacy with Himself after His resurrection.

In His Name

Intimacy with Jesus. *Oneness* with Jesus. What do these words mean except that the union of Christ and His church has engendered a new creation, a new species of man that is part earthborn and part heavenborn. As such, we have access to the presence of God; from here we stand as intercessors for the needs of men. Yet, we also come as God's ambassadors, bringing His Word to men and entreating them on behalf of Christ to be reconciled to God.

So Jesus promises to provide "…whatever you ask of the Father in My name…" (John 15:16). The key to unlocking His promise is the phrase "in My name." The fact is, all of God's promises are accessed through the name of Jesus.

Jesus's name is His divine and kingly seal, His signature on our marching orders. As we are one with Him in intimacy, so we become one with Him in purpose. He said, "…as the Father has sent Me, I also send you" (John 20:21). Thus our prayer is more truly Christ's prayer expressed through us to the Father.

As those whom Christ has commissioned and sent forth in the redemptive purpose, we approach God as Christ's earthly representatives. His "name" is synonymous with His mission, which is to see the lost of this world saved, the wounded healed, and the demonized delivered.

Once, I asked a new secretary to call a certain church leader who is a good friend of mine. She called, but because the individual was very busy, she was unable to get through. After reporting back to me that she could not reach him, I asked her if she had mentioned to my friend's secretary that she was calling for Francis Frangipane. She had not. So I told her to call again using my name. This time she was immediately put through, for he was expecting my call. She gained access, not on the basis of her relationship with him, but through *my* relationship with him. What she presented to him were not her needs and requests but mine. The information my secretary sought was granted because she came in my name representing my purpose.

Likewise, we come to God through Jesus's perfect relationship with Him. On the highest level, we come representing Christ, not ourselves. To the degree we come to God with Jesus's thoughts and motives, we receive power to fulfill Jesus's purpose.

Using the name of Jesus in prayer does not mean I can ask for and receive anything I desire, except where my desires are conformed to the desires of Christ. In other words, I cannot simply attach a religious postscript, "in Jesus's name," at the end of a selfish prayer and expect to always be answered. No. Not until our hearts become purely motivated with Christ's purposes will our prayers return empowered with heaven's resources.

What about our personal needs? Our greatest personal need is to know Jesus. It is here in our intimacy with Christ and His Word that all we need for ourselves is supplied. Did not Jesus say that if we sought first for God's kingdom, all we would ever need on Earth would be added to us (Matt. 6:33)? You see, our confidence in prayer comes from Christ's relationship with the Father, while our joy in life comes from our relationship with Christ.

> Whether we are approaching God's throne in Christ's redemptive purpose or assaulting the strongholds of hell in Christ's eternal judgment, we come in the name of Jesus Christ!

The more we truly come to know Jesus by abiding in Him and His Word abiding in us, we represent Him as we approach the Father in His name. It is here that He assures us: "...ask whatever you wish, and it will be done for you" (John 15:7).

AGAINST THE ENEMY

The expression "in His name" also speaks of the authority Christ has given us in spiritual warfare. We not only represent Christ's interests to the Father, but we also use the authority in His name against the devil and whatever else resists God's revealed purpose. At His name every knee will bow and every tongue confess His lordship.

We are Christ's ambassadors. In the world, those who serve as ambassadors are chosen because of their mastery at representing the interests of their ruler. They have been proven trustworthy; they know the heart of their leader. The most skilled ambassador is one who best represents his lord's intent. Because the emissary continually draws on his leader's instructions, the word of the ambassador becomes as binding as the word of the king himself.

So our oneness with Christ prepares us to mirror His will and to represent His purpose. Whether we are approaching God's throne in Christ's redemptive purpose or assaulting the strongholds of hell in Christ's eternal judgment, we come in the name of Jesus Christ! This is why we can ask whatever we will and it will be granted. We come in the authority of Jesus Christ! Abiding in Jesus's name is our shelter.

What name is like Your name, Lord Jesus? When I speak Your name in worship, it is like honey on my lips; when I utter it in battle, it is a weapon no enemy can oppose. Give me grace, Master, to fully represent You in every aspect of life, to go forth from this moment in the power of Your name! Amen.

Shout joyfully to the LORD, all the earth.

Serve the LORD with gladness;

Come before Him with joyful singing.

Know that the LORD Himself is God;

It is He who has made us, and not we ourselves;

We are His people and the sheep of His pasture.

Enter His gates with thanksgiving

And His courts with praise.

Give thanks to Him, bless His name.

For the LORD is good;

His lovingkindness is everlasting

And His faithfulness to all generations.

—Psalm 100

THIRTEEN

This Time I Will Praise the Lord

WE CANNOT PASS through life without getting hurt. Pain and disappointment in this world are inevitable. But how we handle our setbacks shapes our character and prepares us for eternity. Our attitudes are the pivotal factor determining the level of our immunity from strife.

Regardless of the hardships we have faced, and in spite of the mistakes we have made, the end of our lives can be full of praise and thanksgiving, or full of misery and complaint. In the final analysis, what we have experienced in life will be as rich as the desires we have had fulfilled or as painful as the things we regret.

The Bible tells us, "Hope deferred makes the heart sick" (Prov. 13:12). Those deep disappointments in life have a way of never leaving us. They enter our hearts like fire and then harden into our nature like lava. Setbacks can leave us cautious about new ventures and suspicious of new friends.

Our woundedness restricts our openness. We are fearful we will be hurt again by new relationships. Gradually, unless we learn to handle heartache correctly, we become embittered and resentful cynics. We lose the joy of being alive.

THE SOURCE OF FULFILLMENT

It is our own desires and the degree of their fulfillments that produce either joy or sorrow in our lives. Even basic desires for marriage or friends can enslave us if they consume our attention. Are these desires evil? No. But if having our desires fulfilled is the main reason we have come to Christ, it is possible our lives simply will not improve until our priorities change.

The Lord is concerned about fulfilling our desires, but to do so He must pry our fingers off our lives and turn our hearts toward Him. Indeed, the reason we are alive is not to fulfill our desires, but to become His worshipers.

Personal fulfillment can become an idol; it can develop into such an obsession that we are living for happiness more than living for God. Thus, part of our salvation includes having our desires prioritized by Christ. In the Sermon on the Mount, He put it this way: "But seek first His kingdom and His righteous-ness, and all these things will be added to you. So do not worry about tomorrow; for tomorrow will care for itself..." (Matt. 6:33–34). God wants to, and will, satisfy us beyond our dreams, but not before He is first in our hearts.

Personal fulfillment can become an idol; it can develop into such an obsession that we are living for happiness more than living for God.

A wonderful example of this can be seen in the life of Leah, Jacob's first wife. Leah was unattractive, unwanted, and unloved by her husband. Jacob had served Laban, Leah's father, seven years for Rachel, who was Leah's younger sister. On their wedding night, however, Laban put Leah in the nuptial tent instead of Rachel. Although Jacob actually did marry Rachel a week later, he had to work another seven years for her. So Jacob had two wives who were sisters.

The Scriptures tell us that Rachel was loved by Jacob, but Leah was hated: "And when the LORD saw that Leah was hated..." (Gen. 29:31, KJV).

We must understand this about the nature of God: the Lord is drawn to those who hurt. "The LORD saw...Leah." What wonderful words! In the same way water descends and fills that which is lowest, so Christ reaches first to the afflicted to fill the lowliest and comfort them.

The Lord saw that Leah was unloved. He saw her pain, loneliness, and heartache. Leah, though unloved by Jacob, was deeply loved by the Lord, and He gave her a son. Leah's reaction was predictable. She said, "...surely now my husband will love me" (v. 32).

Worse than living your life alone is to be married to someone who hates you, as was Leah. How Leah wished that Jacob might share the love he had for Rachel with her. Who could blame her? Leah's desires were justified. She had given him a firstborn son. In her mind, if the Lord could open her womb, He could also open Jacob's heart. But the time was not yet; Jacob still did not love her.

Twice more Leah gave birth to sons, and each time her desire was for her husband. She said, "Now this time my husband will become attached to me, because I have borne him three sons" (v. 34). Yet Jacob's heart did not desire her.

For Leah, as well as for us, there is a lesson here: you cannot make another person love you. In fact, the more pressure you place on others to accept you, the more likely they are to reject you instead. Leah's concept of fulfillment was based on attaining Jacob's love, and now her problem was worsening. For not only was she unattractive to Jacob, but her jealousies were also adding to her lack of loveliness.

Three times we read in this text that the Lord saw and heard that Leah was unloved. He had seen her affliction. Through all her striving for Jacob and her disappointment with her marital relationship, the Lord was tenderly wooing Leah to Himself.

DISCOVER GOD'S LOVE

As Leah became pregnant a fourth time, a miracle of grace occurred within her. She gradually became aware that, while she had not been the focus of her husband's love, she was loved by God. And as this fourth pregnancy drew near to completion, she drew nearer and nearer to God. She became a worshiper of the Almighty.

Now as she gave birth to another son, she said, "This time I will praise the LORD" (v. 35). She named that child Judah, which means "praise." It was from the tribe of Judah that Christ was born.

Leah had been seeking self-fulfillment and found only heartache and pain. But as she became a worshiper of God, she entered life's highest fulfillment: she began to please God.

It is right here that the human soul truly begins to change and enter God's shelter. As she found fulfillment in God, He began to remove from her the jealousies, insecurities, and heartaches that life had conveyed to her. A true inner beauty started growing in Leah; she became a woman at rest.

Likewise, we each have character defects that we are reluctant or unable to face. Others have seen these things in us, but they have lacked the courage to tell us. Both physically and personally, these flaws in our nature are what leave us anxious, threatened, and unfulfilled.

It is not counsel or classes on success or self-esteem that we need; we simply need to discover God's love for us. As we begin to praise Him in all things, we simultaneously put on the garments of salvation. We are actually being saved from that which would otherwise have destroyed us!

Disappointments and heartaches cannot cling to us, for we are worshipers of God! And, "God causes all things to work together for good to those who love God" (Rom. 8:28). If we continue to love God, nothing we experience can ultimately turn out harmful!

THE TREE OF LIFE

You will remember the verse we quoted, "Hope deferred makes the heart sick…" (Prov. 13:12). The verse concludes with, "…but desire fulfilled is a tree of life." As our desires are fulfilled, we are fulfilled. Since it is the fulfillment of our desires that fills us with satisfaction, the secret to a rewarding life is to commit our desires to God.

Let Him choose the times and means of our fulfillment, allowing the Lord to prepare us for Himself along the way. The truth is that in ourselves we are incomplete, but in Christ we have been made complete (Col. 2:10).

You say, "That's easy for you to say. You have a wonderful wife and family. You are blessed. But you don't understand my problems." Yes, I do. My wonderful marriage was very difficult for the first few years. We struggled with many things in our relationship. My wife and I both came to the place where we were unfulfilled in each other. But like Leah, we both looked to God and said, "This time I will praise the Lord." In fact, we named our second child the very name that Leah gave to her fourth—Judah.

For us, as for Leah, our lives were turned around as we chose to delight in God in spite of being unfulfilled with each other. As we became His worshipers, He began to work on our hearts until we were not only more pleasing to Him but also pleasing to each other! What I am relating to you is the very thing that saved and blessed our marriage!

> The secret to a rewarding life is to commit our desires to God. Let Him choose the times and means of our fulfillment, allowing the Lord to prepare us for Himself along the way.

Psalm 37:4 states, "Delight yourself in the LORD; and He will give you the desires of your heart." As you delight in God, you change. The negative effects of disappointment and grief fall off. As love and joy from God begin to fulfill us, our very souls are restored and beautified. Yes, delight yourself with Jesus and your self-destructive tendencies will actually begin to vanish. Christ will beautify your life from the inside out.

THE OUTCOME OF LEAH'S LIFE

What happened with Leah? Well, the long years came and went. In time, Rachel and then Leah died. Jacob, on his deathbed, spoke to his sons: "I am about to be gathered to my people; bury me with my fathers in the cave...which Abraham bought...for a burial site. There they buried Abraham and his wife Sarah, there they buried Isaac and his wife Rebekah, and there I buried Leah" (Gen. 49:29–31).

Jacob had buried Leah in the ancestral place of honor! Oh, how those words, though few, say so much! They tell us that God had beautified this afflicted one with salvation. After Leah found fulfillment in God, He gave her fulfillment in Jacob. Over the years, inner peace and spiritual beauty shone forth from Leah; Jacob was knit to her in love. It is not hard to imagine that when Leah died, she left smiling with the praises of God on her lips.

Become a worshiper of God! As you surrender your desires to Him, as you put Him first, He will take what you give Him and make it beautiful in its time. He will take what has been bent and imbalanced within you and make you stand upright in His light and glory.

Therefore, this day speak to your soul. Tell the areas of unfulfillment within you that this time you will praise the Lord!

> *Lord, I am a Leah, unlovely and always seeking the love of those who have rejected me. How foolish I have been—how blind! There is no love, no fulfillment in this life apart from You. You are the tree of life that satisfies all desires; You are the healer of my heart. I love You, Lord Jesus. Amen.*

Offer to God a sacrifice of thanksgiving

And pay your vows to the Most High;

Call upon Me in the day of trouble;

I shall rescue you, and you will honor Me.

—Psalm 50:14–15

FOURTEEN

A Thankful Heart

T HE VERY QUALITY of your life, whether you love it or hate it, is based on how thankful you are toward God. Your attitude determines whether life to you is a place of blessedness or wretchedness and misery. Indeed, looking at the same rosebush, some people complain that the roses have thorns while others rejoice that roses come with the thorns! It all depends on your perspective.

This is the only life you will have before you enter eternity. If you want to find joy, you must first find.

117

thankfulness Indeed the one who is thankful for even a little enjoys much. But the unappreciative soul is always miserable, always complaining. He lives outside the shelter of the Most High God.

Perhaps the worst enemy we have is not the devil but our own tongue. James tells us, "The tongue is set among our members as that which...sets on fire the course of our life..." (James 3:6). He goes on to say this fire is ignited by hell. Consider: with our own words we can enter the spirit of heaven or the agonies of hell!

It is hell with its punishments, torments, and miseries that controls the life of the grumbler and complainer! Paul expands this thought in 1 Corinthians 10:10, where he reminds us of the Jews who "grumble[d]...and were destroyed by the destroyer." The fact is, every time we open up to grumbling and complaining, the quality of our life is reduced proportionally—a destroyer is bringing our life to ruin!

People often ask me, "What is the ruling demon over our church or city?" They expect me to answer with the ancient Aramaic or Phoenician name of a fallen angel. What I usually tell them is a lot more practical: one of the most pervasive evil influences over our nation is ingratitude!

Do not minimize the strength and cunning of this enemy! Paul said that the Jews who grumbled and complained during their difficult circumstances were "destroyed by the destroyer." Who was this destroyer? If you insist on discerning an ancient world ruler, one of the most powerful spirits mentioned in the Bible is Abaddon, whose Greek name is Apollyon. It means "destroyer" (Rev. 9:11). Paul said the Jews were destroyed by this spirit. In other words, when we are complaining or unthankful, we open the door to the destroyer, Abaddon, the demon king over the abyss of hell!

IN THE PRESENCE OF GOD

Multitudes in our nation have become specialists in the "science of misery." They are experts—moral accountants who can, in a moment, tally all the wrongs society has ever done to them or their group. I have never talked with one of these people who was happy, blessed, or content about anything. They expect an imperfect world to treat them perfectly.

Truly there are people in this wounded country of ours who need special attention. Most of us, however, simply need to repent of ingratitude, for it is ingratitude itself that is keeping wounds alive! We simply need to forgive the wrongs of the past and become thankful for what we have in the present.

The moment we become grateful, we actually begin to ascend spiritually into the presence of God. The psalmist wrote:

> Serve the LORD with gladness; come before Him with joyful singing....Enter His gates with thanksgiving and His courts with praise. Give thanks to Him, bless His name. For the LORD is good; His lovingkindness is ever-lasting and His faithfulness to all generations.
> —Psalm 100:2, 4–5

It does not matter what your circumstances are; the instant you begin to thank God, even though your situation has not changed, *you* begin to change. The key that unlocks the gates of heaven is a thankful heart. Entrance into the courts of God comes as you simply begin to praise the Lord.

A THANKFUL MAN IS A HUMBLE MAN

If you think you know God but do not live your life in gratitude before Him, it is doubtful that you really do know Him. A thankful heart honors God. Often when we say we "know God," what we really mean is that we know facts about Him. But we should ask ourselves, "Do I truly know *Him*?"

> It does not matter what your circumstances are; the instant you begin to thank God, even though your situation has not changed, you begin to change.

Paul warns that just knowing doctrines about God is not enough to enter eternal life. He said:

> For since the creation of the world His invisible attributes, His eternal power and divine nature, have been clearly seen, being understood through what has been made, so that they are without excuse. For even though they knew God, they did not honor Him as God or give thanks, but

they became futile in their speculations, and their foolish heart was darkened.

—Romans 1:20–21

Even though we may know God, if we do not honor Him as God and thank Him for ruling in our lives, our thoughts turn foolish and our minds darken. When we are in that ungrateful state of mind, every word we speak is a spark lit by hell, set to feed on and consume our joy and hope in this world.

H. W. Beecher said, "Pride slays thanksgiving...a proud man is seldom a grateful man, for he never thinks he gets as much as he deserves."* We should be thankful that we do not get what we deserve, for each of us deserves hell! When adversities or the small irritations of life come your way, be thankful you are not getting what you deserve!

The truth is, God's plan allows for problems so He can teach us to "Rejoice always; pray without ceasing; in everything give thanks; for this is God's will for you in Christ Jesus" (1 Thess. 5:16–18). Are small irritations God's will? No. Rejoicing in the difficulty is God's will, and remaining thankful during the crisis is God's will.

It is obvious that the Lord does not want us to succumb to defeat, for it is His will that we "pray without ceasing."

He did not say, "Accept the difficulties." He said to pray,

---

* Henry Ward Beecher, *Life Thoughts: Gathered From the Extemporaneous Discourses of Henry Ward Beecher*, ed. Edna Dean Proctor (Boston: Phillips, Sampson and Company, 1858), 115.

continue to rejoice, and remain vocally thankful. As you do, your circumstances will be established in victory!

This very thing happened to me during a time of great difficulty in the beginning of my ministry. I was battling with poverty, disappointment, and the struggle of guiding our congregation's growth. I knew I was at a crossroads. But as long as I thought I deserved more, I was not thankful for what the Lord had given me.

When God gives us less than we desire, it is not because He is teaching us poverty; He is teaching us thankfulness.

You see, life—real life—is not based on what we amass but on what we enjoy. In those very circumstances God had given me much to appreciate, but I could not see it because my heart was wrong. Once I repented and simply began to enjoy the church He had given me, my whole life changed.

God wants us to be blessed and to prosper with the real things of life. If we are distracted by comparing ourselves to other churches or other people, however, how can we appreciate what He has given us? We simply need to be grateful.

> The Lord does not want us to succumb to defeat. He did not say, "Accept the difficulties." He said to pray, continue to rejoice, and remain vocally thankful.

Someone once said, "When I see a poor man who is grateful, I know if he were rich, he would be generous." A thankful spirit is akin to a generous spirit, for both appreciate and receive the riches of God. When we are thankful with little, God can entrust us with much.

OUT OF ZION GOD HAS SHOWN FORTH

> The Mighty One, God, the LORD, has spoken, and summoned the earth from the rising of the sun to its setting. Out of Zion, the perfection of beauty, God has shone forth.
>
> —Psalm 50:1–2

God shines forth out of Zion. It is this God, beautifying His creation with His presence, who calls His people into covenant union. To accomplish the glorification of His people, the Lord calls, "Gather My godly ones to Me, those who have made a covenant with Me by sacrifice" (Ps. 50:5).

To make a covenant with someone is to enjoin ourselves in the most solemn bonds of unity. As we said earlier, a covenant is more than a promise; it is the pledge of two lives to live as one. The union God seeks with us is called a covenant of sacrifice.

This covenant is not a ritual form of worship; it is not the Jewish sacrifice of bulls and goats. It transcends time and methodology and reaches to every soul who longs for the living God. It is a covenant of thanksgiving. God says:

> Gather My godly ones to Me, those who have made a covenant with Me by sacrifice.... I know every bird of the mountains, and everything that moves in the field is

Mine.... Offer to God a sacrifice of thanksgiving and pay
your vows to the Most High.... He who offers a sacrifice
of thanksgiving honors Me; and to him who orders his
way aright I shall show the salvation of God.
—Psalm 50:5, 11, 14, 23

The terms of the covenant are simple: We pledge to thank
Him and adore Him in everything. He pledges to shine forth
from our lives in the perfection of beauty. It is a sacrifice of
thanksgiving, for it will cost us to praise Him when we hurt. But
to do so is part of our healing and the beginning of our salvation. Begin to thank Him. Name the gifts He has given to you,
starting with the blessing of life itself. When we thank Him, we
are honoring Him.

Today God is calling for His people to enter into a covenant
bond with Him—a covenant where we pledge to live a thankful
life and He pledges His life to shine forth through us. This covenant of thanksgiving is the key that shuts and bolts the door to
demonic oppression in a person's life. It is a glorious gate into the
shelter of the Most High God.

*Blessed Lord, forgive me for being a complainer. Help me
to offer to You the sacrifice of thanksgiving in all things.
Lord, I come this day to make a covenant with You. By
Your grace, I will be thankful regardless of what my life
seems to be. O God, remember Your covenant pledge and
gather me near to Your heart. In Jesus's name, amen.*

"Can the prey be taken from the mighty man,

Or the captives of a tyrant be rescued?"

Surely, thus says the LORD,

"Even the captives of the mighty man will be taken away,

And the prey of the tyrant will be rescued;

For I will contend with the one who contends with you,

And I will save your sons.

I will feed your oppressors with their own flesh,

And they will become drunk with their own blood as with

sweet wine;

And all flesh will know that I, the LORD, am your Savior

And your Redeemer, the Mighty One of Jacob."

—Isaiah 49:24–26

FIFTEEN

THE VALLEY OF FRUITFULNESS

THE BATTLES WE face are often intense times of weakness, distress, and confusion. If the events of our lives were charted, these would be the lowest points. Yet God is no less with us during difficulties than at other times. In fact, these valleys are often as much the plan of God as our mountaintop experiences.

There is a story in the Bible that speaks plainly to this truth. Israel had recently defeated the Arameans in a mountain battle. In 1 Kings 20, we read:

Then the prophet came near to the king of Israel and said to him, "Go, strengthen yourself and observe and see what you have to do; for at the turn of the year the king of Aram will come up against you." Now the servants of the king of Aram said to him, "Their gods are gods of the mountains, therefore they were stronger than we; but rather let us fight against them in the plain, and surely we will be stronger than they."

—1 Kings 20:22–23

The enemy said that the God of Israel was a god of the mountains, but if they fought the Jews in the valleys they would defeat them. We read in verse 28:

Then a man of God came near and spoke to the king of Israel and said, "Thus says the LORD, 'Because the Arameans have said, "The LORD is a god of the mountains, but He is not a god of the valleys," therefore I will give all this great multitude into your hand, and you shall know that I am the LORD.'"

—1 Kings 20:28

No matter what the enemy tries to tell you, Christ is God of the mountains *and* God of the valleys. He has not stopped being God because you happen to be in a valley. He is the God of glory as seen in His power and miracles. In the valleys He reveals Himself as faithful, loyally committed to us in difficulties and distresses. In and through all things He is our God.

When we are on the "mountaintops" of our Christian experience, we can see our future clearly. We have perspective and confidence. When we are in one of life's valleys, however, our vision is limited and our future seems hidden. Yet valleys are also the most fertile places on the earth.

Valleys produce fruitfulness. You can expect there to be a harvest of virtue when God dwells with you in the valleys.

THE HIGHWAY TO ZION

> How blessed is the man whose strength is in You, in whose heart are the highways to Zion! Passing through the valley of Baca they make it a spring.
>
> —Psalm 84:5–6

Baca means "weeping." Each of us has times of weeping when our hearts and hopes seem crushed. Because God has placed in our hearts "highways to Zion," however, we *pass through* valleys; we do not live in them.

"Passing through the valley of Baca..." Once we are on the other side of weeping, our Redeemer makes our valley experience into "a spring." The very things that overwhelmed us will, in time, refresh us with new life. Whether we are experiencing the height of success and power or are in a valley of weakness and despair, the Lord is our God continually!

Has the enemy isolated you, causing you to doubt God's love? Do not forget, while we were yet sinners, Christ died for us. Even the hairs on your head are numbered. He cares. It is His love for us that redeems our hardships and not only brings good out of what was meant for evil, but also trains us to deliver others.

How did Jesus prepare to do wonderful works? Part of His training involved suffering. Christ was a man of sorrows. He was One who was acquainted with grief. Yet His suffering was the

Father's means of acquainting Him with the actual feelings of mankind's need and pain. Because He suffered what we suffer, He is able to serve as a faithful high priest. If we yield to God's plan for Christ to be formed in us, God will take our sorrows to enlarge our hearts. Once we have been acquainted with grief, we then can be anointed with compassion to deliver others.

Joseph's Trials

Consider Joseph. He was the second youngest of Jacob's sons and his father's favorite. His walk with God began with dreams and visions. Joseph's life is a pattern for many who have had a genuine call from God. Our walk with God may also have begun with a "travel brochure" of dreams and visions where God gives us a picture of His destination for us. Yet we fail to be able to see how His promises will come to pass in our lives.

> When we are in one of life's valleys, our vision is limited and our future seems hidden. But no matter what the enemy tries to tell you, Christ is God of the mountains and God of the valleys.

Joseph was betrayed by his brothers and delivered up by them to die. He was unjustly accused when Potiphar's wife tried to seduce him. He was imprisoned and forgotten by all except God, who patiently watched and measured Joseph's reaction to difficulty.

Rich or poor, blessed or smitten, Joseph served God. He was being tested, but he continued to pass his tests. Joseph was on trial before men, but he was found innocent before God.

Finally, at the right moment, the Lord suddenly connected all the loose ends of Joseph's life. Everything that Joseph went through would have seemed cruel and unfair except that the Lord was shaping a man for His purpose. God uses everything we go through for future purposes that He alone sees. We do not see His ultimate plan while we are in the valley. We must remember the vision, keeping faith in what God has promised.

Just as He allowed Joseph to go through many trials, so He allows us to go through great conflicts as well. For He knows that our lives—what we have become through His grace—will help others find the shelter of the Most High God in their lives.

"Joseph named the firstborn Manasseh, 'For,' he said, 'God has made me forget all my trouble and all my father's household'" (Gen. 41:51). God caused Joseph to forget the difficulty and pain of his life. There is something wonderful about the Lord's capacity to cause all things to work for good. With Jesus in our lives, a time ultimately comes when God causes us to forget all the troubles of the past.

"He named the second Ephraim, 'For,' he said, 'God has made me fruitful in the land of my affliction'" (Gen. 41:52). God made him fruitful in the very things that afflicted him. In the land of your affliction, in your battle, is the place where God will make you fruitful.

131

Consider even now the area of greatest affliction in your life. In that area God will make you fruitful in such a way that your heart will be fully satisfied and God's heart fully glorified. Ultimately, the Lord will touch many others with the substance of what you have gained. In a world that is superficial, Christ will produce something within you that is deep and living.

God has not promised to keep us from valleys and sufferings, but He *has* promised to make us fruitful in them. Without a doubt we each will pass through valleys before we reach our final goal in God. As we remain faithful to Him in trials, the character and nature of Christ Jesus will emerge in our spirits; and Christ will be revealed to those around us. He intends to make your life a key that unlocks God's shelter for others.

> Consider even now the area of greatest affliction in your life. In that area God will make you fruitful in such a way that your heart will be fully satisfied and God's heart fully glorified.

Lord, You are God of the mountains and the valleys. I know that Your faithfulness is my shield and my bulwark.

Thank You for redeeming the conflicts of my life. I praise You for healing me and causing me to forget all the trauma of my past. Now, Lord, help me to remember what I have learned. Cause me to remember that the crises in my life always precede the enrichment of my life. Help me to recognize that the place of my fruitfulness is in the land of my affliction. In Jesus's name, amen.

Be kind to one another, tender-hearted, forgiving each other,

just as God in Christ also has forgiven you. Therefore be

imitators of God, as beloved children; and walk in love, just as

Christ also loved you and gave Himself up for us, an offering

and a sacrifice to God as a fragrant aroma.

—Ephesians 4:32–5:2

SIXTEEN

A Forgiving Heart

DURING THE LAST hours of this age, there will be two opposing factions in the world: those whose hearts are wrought with bitterness, resentment, and hatred; and those whose love has actually increased and who are experiencing the power of the kingdom of God. Jesus foretold these conditions in Matthew: "At that time many will fall away and will betray one another and hate one another.... Because lawlessness [iniquity] is increased, most people's love will grow cold" (Matt. 24:10, 12).

But then He added: "This gospel of the kingdom shall be preached in the whole world as a testimony to all the nations, and then the end will come" (v. 14).

What is this "gospel of the kingdom"? It is the whole truth that Jesus came to bring—not only that which saves us from our sins, but also that which creates us in His image. It is the full gospel with all its requirements and all its rewards—the full price for the full power. It is the most glorious pearl that man can possess: the presence of God in glory revealed within and among us.

Thus if we are to attain this great love, we will continually be forced to make the choice between mercy and unforgiveness. If we do not walk in a forgiving attitude, we will certainly become prey to an embittered spirit. If it is indeed God's plan to allow wickedness and holiness to grow simultaneously to full maturity, then we must guard our hearts beforehand from reacting in bitterness and unforgiveness. The increasing lawlessness will certainly give us occasions to lose love.

Yet just to survive in this cruel world, we often withdraw from the vulnerability of love. We cannot choose cautious, selective love and also walk in the power of God's kingdom. To counter pain, we unconsciously shut down our love, for it is love that makes us vulnerable. God wants us to be a people whose love is growing hot, not cold.

Jesus did not say we had to trust our enemies, but He did say that we had to love them. You ask, "Why?" One reason God allows difficulties is to test us. He wants to see if our Christianity is merely an intellectual pursuit or if following Him is truly the highest passion of our hearts. Thus He tells us to "love your enemies and pray for those who persecute you" (Matt. 5:44).

Some of you have gone through rejection and betrayal, but the Lord says you did not fail. You have continued to love. Although you went through great pain, you have forgiven those who have hurt you. You passed the test.

> What is this "gospel of tho kingdom"? It is the whole truth that Jesus came to bring—not only that which saves us from our sins, but also that which creates us in His image.

Some of us still have certain individuals in our lives whom we have not forgiven and whom we do not love. Perhaps you are right; they do not deserve your forgiveness. But what you do not realize is the consequence of your anger.

LIVE IN THE HERE AND NOW

As long as you refuse to forgive, a part of you is trapped in the past where you are continually being reminded of your pain. Even the calendar season in which you were hurt stimulates depression and foreboding! Until you forgive, you will not be fully released to go on with your life.

There is only one way we can have true fellowship with God, and that is in the "here and now." But when your mind is harboring unforgiveness, you are neither in the "here" nor in the "now." When you live in the past, you are cut off from God. What they did to you is over. It is done. It does not have any real existence or life of its own except in your mind.

There within you the conflict continues to live. And as long as it lives, you are still being hurt by it. The person who wounded you may have long since died. That person cannot be blamed, for you are the one who keeps your wounds alive!

> If you do not forgive those who have hurt you, you will lose a measure of your capacity to love. Whether they deserve forgiveness or not, you deserve a better life!

Not only is the quality of your spiritual life affected, but your physical well-being pays a price as well. As long as you keep holding on to the burden of what someone did to you, each time you think about that person your stomach acids churn and your anxiety increases. Your body is continually put under stress.

CHOOSE TO LOVE

If you do not forgive those who have hurt you, you will lose a measure of your capacity to love. Whether they deserve forgiveness or not, you deserve a better life! And God wants to give you a better life. But you cannot enjoy abundant life while carrying unforgiveness, for you are shackled to something that hurt you, and your own unforgiveness tortures you.

How do you get out of that prison? How do you find the protection of God for your soul? God calls you to forgive. You must see the hands of God reaching to you in the midst of your pain. He wants to redeem that conflict, using that specific adversity to perfect character in you. It will be this event that He will use to make you like Christ.

Each time you say, "Father, I choose to love; I choose to forgive; I choose to forget and to not hold bitterness and unforgiveness against that person," you are taking on Christ's nature. Rejoice! Jesus is taking over your heart! You are entering the shelter of the Most High God.

> *Master, I see in Your forgiveness of me the pattern for my forgiveness of others. Lord, You forgave the Pharisees who lied about You; You pardoned the soldiers who mocked and crucified You; You encouraged Your disciples' hearts to not be troubled, knowing they were about to deny and betray You.*
>
> *Yet, You not only forgave them, but You also died for them. You opened Your heart as wide as the universe and welcomed all to be reconciled to God. Grant me the power to forgive, to lay down my life for others, and to know the love that compelled You to such righteousness! Amen.*

Beloved, let us love one another, for love is from God; and everyone who loves is born of God and knows God. The one who does not love does not know God, for God is love.... We have come to know and have believed the love which God has for us. God is love, and the one who abides in love abides in God, and God abides in him. By this, love is perfected with us, so that we may have confidence in the day of judgment; because as He is, so also are we in this world.

—1 John 4:7–8, 16 17

SEVENTEEN

LOVE: GOD'S PRESERVATIVE

THERE WILL BE a time when each of us will stand before Jesus Christ and He will open a door called "reality past." There we shall gaze into the days of our earthly existence. Jesus will not only commend our lives in a general way, but He will also point to specific things we did. Rejoicing together with us, He will say, "Well done!" Perhaps there was a special act of kindness that turned a bitter person back toward God, or perhaps you overcame your fears and led a person to Christ whom God then used to win thousands.

In the Latin translation of the Bible, the phrase "well done" is rendered "Bravo!" How would you like Jesus to say that to you? Imagine Him with His arm around your shoulder, saying, "Bravo! You were just an average person, but you trusted Me; you learned to love without fear. Look how many hearts we touched together!" To be so pleasing to Christ that He rejoices over the life we give Him should be our highest goal.

LOVE IN THE MIDST OF PRESSURE

Yet, it is here, in a world filled with devils, devil-possessed people, and conflicts of all sorts, that we must find the life of Christ. In fact, Jesus warned about the Great Tribulation; one meaning of the word *tribulation* is "pressure." Even today, is not stress and pressure increasing on people? In spite of these tensions God has called us to love extravagantly. If we do not counteract the stress of this age with love, we will crumble beneath the weight of offenses.

> To be so pleasing to Christ that He rejoices over the life we give Him should be our highest goal.

Have you ever seen a supermarket shopping cart full of bent food cans? Most have lost their labels. You can buy a half dozen for a dollar or two. Often what has happened is that the atmospheric pressure outside the can was greater than the pressure inside and the can collapsed. It could not withstand the pressure.

Similarly, we must have an aggressive force pushing from the inside out that is equal to the pressures trying to crumble us from the outside. We need the pressure of God's love pouring out through us, neutralizing the pressures of hatred and bitterness in the world.

Love is God's preservative. It surrounds our souls with a power greater than the power of the devil and the world around us. It keeps us balanced. It insulates us against the hostility that exists in our world. Love *is* the shelter of the Most High; it is the substance of God's stronghold.

Lord, forgive me for looking for some other means of protection besides Your love. Truly, pressures have increased on my life; stress multiplies daily in my world. Lord, grant me the eternal equalizer: love.

Grant that I would walk in such surrender to You that the power of Your love would unceasingly emanate from my soul. Amen.

Behold, how happy is the man whom God reproves, so do not despise the discipline of the Almighty. For He inflicts pain, and gives relief; He wounds, and His hands also heal. From six troubles He will deliver you, even in seven evil will not touch you. In famine He will redeem you from death, and in war from the power of the sword. You will be hidden from the scourge of the tongue, and you will not be afraid of violence when it comes. You will laugh at violence and famine, and you will not be afraid of wild beasts. For you will be in league with the stones of the field, and the beasts of the field will be at peace with you. You will know that your tent is secure, for you will visit your abode and fear no loss. You will know also that your descendants will be many, and your offspring as the grass of the earth. You will come to the grave in full vigor, like the stacking of grain in its season. Behold this; we have investigated it, and so it is. Hear it, and know for yourself.

—Job 5:17–27

EIGHTEEN

PROTECTED FROM THE ACCUSER

How do you handle criticism? How does one protect himself from the "scourge of the tongue" (Job 5:21)? Where is the stronghold from accusation? If you are going to be successful in the Lord's work, you must find God's hiding place from one of the most painful weapons in Satan's arsenal: the critical tongue.

The fact is, for better or for worse, people are going to talk about you. You cannot do the will of God without causing changes, and changes will always cause some to stumble.

151

In fact, Jesus said we were to beware when all men speak well of us. He said we cannot serve two masters; if we are to truly please Him, we cannot be distracted by trying to please everyone else.

At the same time, there is a demonic strategy that is set against those who teach God's Word and minister to His people. The enemy's campaign is not only aimed at destroying the shepherd; he also seeks to scatter the sheep. If Satan's attack is successful, everyone involved will come out of the battle with less love and a hardened heart.

I find it amazing that individuals can react so differently to the same teaching. One will be uplifted and encouraged while another may not only miss the Lord's blessing, but also actually be offended by an isolated statement.

It seems that for every person who takes the hammer and chisel to make an idol of a preacher, there is someone else with a hammer and spikes ready to crucify him. Unless that man is sustained by the Lord, the pressures against him can be overwhelming.

Most people fail to remember that a minister is just like any other Christian. He is not Superman; bullets (and words) do not bounce off his chest. He is not invulnerable to cruel and malicious talk. He is an imperfect person called to serve the living God in the body of Christ, but he is nonetheless just a person.

For most, church is a place where people go to express their worship of God, to be taught, and to have fellowship. But to the man or woman of God, the church is God's garden. Most of the real work a pastor does is not in the pulpit but in the unheralded service of cultivating love and trust in personal relationships.

In God's eyes, the church is much more than a meeting place of casual acquaintances or doctrinally united believers. To the Father, the church is a living temple, a human house for the Spirit of His Son. The Bible says that when He placed us in our particular church, it actually gave Him pleasure (1 Cor. 12:18). Together with the Holy Spirit, the pastor and elders work to bring the church into a right relationship with God's love and then to spread that love throughout the entire citywide church.

> Most people fail to remember that a minister is just like any other Christian. He is not Superman; bullets (and words) do not bounce off his chest. He is an imperfect person called to serve the living God in the body of Christ.

God has provided honorable ways for people to transfer from one church to another. If someone wants to leave a church to start their own, there are proper ways to receive God's anointing and be sent. (See Acts 13:1–3.) It is not necessary to find fault and cause a church split. When things are done correctly and in order, people are edified.

But when relationships are severed and destroyed through malicious gossip, or when a developing trust is turned into mistrust through backbiting and criticism, God Himself is angered (Prov. 6:16–19). And if God is offended, how much more difficult is it for His servants to remain aloof from the conflict that sin causes.

THE ANSWER

So how does a man or woman of God find the balance between his basic need to survive and his responsibility to please God? The answer is to put on Christ's love.

A number of years ago I went through a difficult time during which a handful of people made me the target of ongoing criticism. There is a type of constructive criticism coming through people who love you that teaches and helps you to prosper, and there is a type of criticism that comes through an embittered spirit that is not meant to correct you but to destroy you. It was the latter relationship that I had with these people.

To be honest, I am sure that there were areas in my life that were out of balance; some of their complaints were justified. Much of what they had to say, however, was said to others behind my back. Our congregation was being destabilized by these individuals. Try as I did, nothing I could say or repent of would silence them.

For three years I sought the Lord, yet He would not vindicate me of their accusations. Instead, He dealt with me. He reached deep into the very substructure of my soul and began to touch hidden areas of my life.

At issue with the Lord was not my sin, but my "self." The Bible says our sins are ever before us (Ps. 51:3); these I could see. But I had no perspective on my own soul. The Lord allowed this criticism to continue until it unearthed something deeper and more fundamentally wrong than any of my doctrinal interpretations or sins. It unearthed me.

The Holy Spirit began to show me how easily I was manipulated by people's criticisms, and especially how much my sense of peace was governed by the acceptance or rejection of man. As much as I prayed, God would not deliver me from my enemy. He saved me by killing that part of me that was vulnerable to the devil, and He did it with the accusations themselves.

I will never forget the day it dawned on me that both God and the devil wanted me to die, but for different reasons. Satan wanted to destroy me through slander and then drain me with the unceasing activity of explaining "my side" to people. At the same time, God wanted to crucify that part of my soul that was so easily exploited by the devil in the first place!

It was a pivotal day when I realized that this battle was not going to be over until I died to what people said about me. It was probably at this point when I finally and truly became a servant of God.

Today I stand in awe of what the Lord did during those terrible yet wonderful months. He knew a time would come when the things I wrote would touch the lives of millions of people. To inoculate me from the praise of man, He baptized me in the criticism of man until I died to the control of man.

Do not misunderstand me; I still honestly pray about things submitted to me by others, and I am accountable to other leaders. I even have staff people whose assignment is to give me a critical analysis of my life and work. But I am no longer ruled by man.

I live for God's pleasure, and if I happen to please man, that is His business, not mine.

THE SHELTER OF HIS CROSS

There is something utterly marvelous about the Lord's redemptive powers. No matter what hardship, devilish plot, or accusation is hurled our way, everything Satan would use to destroy is redeemed by God's love; then it is used to perfect us. If we faithfully seek the Lord, adversity becomes like gasoline on our hearts' fire for God. Just to survive, we are driven deeper into the blaze of His presence.

Thus, as much as I hated it when people slandered me, this was the very thing God used to compel me nearer to His heart. As important as Bible study and church attendance are, it was adversity that worked the deepest death of self and brought me closest to God. I have come to sincerely love and appreciate my enemies—I could not have come to this place of blessedness without them!

> No matter what hardship, devilish plot, or accusation is hurled our way, everything Satan would use to destroy is redeemed by God's love; then it is used to perfect us.

I can see why Jesus said, "Blessed are those who have been persecuted for the sake of righteousness, for theirs is the kingdom of heaven" (Matt. 5:10). Certainly He does not mean that we experience "heaven" outwardly when we are persecuted or suffer mental or physical abuse. No. But inwardly God deals mightily with our souls, breaking the addiction to man's approval and liberating us to truly live for Christ.

In His wisdom, God gives us two gifts: a new nature and a cross uniquely designed to kill our old nature. The moment we begin to pick up the cross, we enter the shelter of God.

We must learn this truth: God does not want our old nature to survive. He does not want us to reform that which actually needs to be crucified; He wants it to die. Not only was our old nature corrupt and indefensible against the enemy, but also the flesh is akin to the devil and most easily inhabited by him.

The character of the new nature, however, is Christ Himself. With the living Christ within me, how will I bring a charge against my neighbor, for Christ commands me to love? If I issue a complaint, will I raise my old nature from the dead to be my witness? Will I silence Christ to hear the voice of the accuser?

You see, if I am to be the Lord's servant, when I am offended I must repeat Christ's prayer from the cross: "Father, forgive them; for they do not know what they are doing" (Luke 23:34).

So, regardless of man's opinions about us, whether we are exalted or abased, let us determine to carry Christ's cross throughout the conflict. For these momentary light afflictions are producing for us an eternal weight of glory far beyond all comparison.

My personal attitude is this: I will stand for revival, unity, and prayer; and I will labor to restore healing and reconciliation between God's people. Yet if all God truly wanted was to raise up one fully yielded son—a son who refused to be offended, refused to react, and refused to harbor unforgiveness, regardless of those who slander and persecute—I have determined to be that person. My primary goal in all things is not revival but to bring pleasure to Christ.

None of us are there yet. But if we each have this attitude, we will put to death our reactions to criticisms and offenses.

And though we may still stumble, we will learn that carrying the cross is not merely dying to self; it is embracing the love of Christ that forgives the very ones who have crucified us.

> *Lord, help me to hear with humility the criticisms of those who accuse me. Grant me peace to prosper spiritually when others find fault. Yet even more than this, help me to die to all I was and live to all You are. I desperately want to be found in Your nature and to be changed into Your image. Amen.*

The LORD is my light and my salvation;

Whom shall I fear?

The LORD is the defense of my life;

Whom shall I dread?

When evildoers came upon me to devour my flesh,

My adversaries and my enemies, they stumbled and fell.

Though a host encamp against me,

My heart will not fear;

Though war arise against me,

In spite of this I shall be confident.

One thing I have asked from the LORD, that I shall seek:

That I may dwell in the house of the LORD all the days of

my life,

To behold the beauty of the LORD

And to meditate in His temple.

For in the day of trouble He will conceal me in His tabernacle;

In the secret place of His tent He will hide me;

He will lift me up on a rock.

—Psalm 27:1–5

NINETEEN

At the Throne With God

THERE IS A time when, having been touched by God, something truly of Christ is conceived in your spirit. It is actually a time when the hopes of God begin to fill your imagination and dreams. The experience is very much like a pregnancy; that which God has conceived within you is now being nurtured by your faith and protected through your prayers. Christ is being formed within you (Gal. 4:19). From this time on, your walk with God is never merely a religion—it is a destiny.

Yet, at this stage of our development, spiritual immaturity is unavoidable. It takes time for the promise of God to gestate within us. We struggle with impatience and anxiety. We think that on our own initiative we can attain all that God has promised. If we accept delays, we are harassed by guilt.

BIRTHING THE PROMISE OF GOD

It takes time before we finally realize that only God can fulfill what He has promised. Our task is to cooperate with Him in the preparation of our hearts. Thus the first stages of our walks with Christ are usually not times of fulfillment but development.

But the Almighty is not the only supernatural personality intently watching our lives. Satan also senses the sacredness and destiny of the life that is growing within us. Especially as our time of fulfillment actually draws near, the devil seeks to abort the work of God within us. We face battles inside and out. In the dark hours of the night we question our motives and doubt our readiness.

Externally we face the accusations of the people Satan uses to accuse or criticize our actions. We react wrongly to those whose attitudes Satan manipulates. We argue our case before them: "Something of God is in me! Don't you see? Don't criticize me; help me!"

Yet, rarely do we find comfort seeking the approval of men, and what comfort we find is fleeting. Will we blame men for their apparent lack of support? No. For by divine decree, no one can truly supply us with the support we crave except the Lord

Himself. Even though we may owe our very spiritual existence to the intercessory prayer of another, what God conceives within us ultimately must find its strength in Christ alone.

You will remember that when Solomon built the temple, he had inscribed on its two pillars the names Jachin and Boaz (1 Kings 7:21). *Jachin* means "He will establish." *Boaz* means "in Him is strength." If we will enter and abide in true service to God, we must abandon reliance on any strength but His or any success except what He establishes.

PRAYER BEGETS BREAKTHROUGH

Revelation 12 provides insight into the pattern of true spiritual growth. We see here a depiction of Christ's inception within us. It is followed by the gestation period of preparation and the attempt of Satan to abort the emergence of Christ in our lives. Finally, we see the manifestation of Christ's nature revealed and functional through His human servant.

> It we will enter and abide in true service to God, we must abandon reliance on any strength but His or any success except what He establishes.

John saw a great sign: "...a woman clothed with the sun, and the moon under her feet, and on her head a crown of twelve stars; and she was with child..." (Rev. 12:1–2).

Various commentators see this woman as Israel birthing Christ, or the saints of both covenants becoming the new Israel. Others see the process whereby God moves people through prayer to release great spiritual awakenings among the nations. Still others see a type of the extraordinary intercession of saints at the end of the age, whose travail consummates itself in Christ's return.

Whatever the travailing woman in Revelation 12 signifies, our primary focus is on the principle we see underlying her activity. Mirrored in this woman's pain is the reflection, on a much smaller scale, of our own struggle to see Christ truly birthed in our service to God.

Without minimizing the importance of good works or faithfulness to our current task, there is a time when something deep within us demands that we rise to meet our approaching destiny with extraordinary prayer. It is a time when a new dimension of Christ is about to emerge in our lives.

The woman in labor has carried God's purposes to the point of breakthrough. The energy she expended in all her former works fuses into one great labor of prayer: "...she cried out, being in labor and in pain to give birth" (v. 2). In this deep intercession, she gives birth to one who will "...rule all the nations with a rod of iron" (v. 5).

So also it is with us. The vision God has put in our spirits may not rule the entire world, but when it emerges, it will be Christ; He will rule our world. He cannot come forth, however, apart from our faith, preparation, and travailing prayer.

There is a time to work, serve, and be seen. There is another time when the purpose of God within us is at hand. This is a time for focused prayer.

It is significant that in recent years the Lord has led the church into greater, more fervent prayer. There is nothing less noble about the works of the Lord, but a new purpose is about to be born. It is time to pray.

THE ENEMY'S ASSAULT

If all there was to launching a new move of God was prayer, we would by now be in revival. But as John's vision reveals, the woman in Revelation 12 was about to give birth when there appeared another sign: "A great red dragon...stood before the woman...so that when she gave birth he might devour her child. And she gave birth to a son, a male child..." (vv. 3–5).

> There is a time to work, serve, and be seen. There is another time when the purpose of God within us is at hand. This is a time for focused prayer.

Most believe this one who was born to the woman represents the person and work of Jesus Christ. Yet even the Son of God began His life as a small and defenseless baby.

Likewise, everyone whom God has ever used—everything God has ever done since the fall of Adam—has entered the world in a vulnerable condition and in need of protection. It is while the new work of God is trembling forward that Satan seeks to bring his greatest assault. The form he takes in his war against our new beginnings in Christ is accusation.

It is during this time that God's purpose for us is most vulnerable. The dragon that positioned itself at the womb of the woman is, in the same chapter, revealed as the devil, specifically identified as the accuser of the brethren.

THE POWER OF WORDS

When the devil accuses us, he does not come with accusations that are without some measure of truth. He points out our littleness, emphasizes our lack of spirituality, exploits our ignorance and fears, and condemns us for our immaturity and failures. Using mere words, he halts, or at least hinders, our new beginnings.

Recall your first witness to someone about Christ or perhaps the first time you spoke in a Bible study. For many, a flood of words stormed against their heart afterward: "Did you really say that? No one listened! You didn't sound as though you knew what you were saying! They didn't care about your message; you just turned them off!"

Those words came from the accuser of the brethren. Because of this spirit, the purpose of God has been aborted in many Christians. Many who ought to be in awe of the Spirit of Christ within them have settled instead for a mere theology about Jesus Christ. Thus Satan exploited their imperfections and buried their hope of Christ under a barrage of accusation.

Even if the accuser has successfully hindered you in this regard, know this with certainty: Christ in you cannot die. He only awaits a new mixture of hope with faith and prayer with perseverance. The enemy you are fighting is not failure, ignorance, or lack of spirituality. Your enemy is the accuser of the brethren. He seeks to manipulate your shortcomings and use them against you. Through a flood of words, he wants to reduce your relationship with God to a hollow religion, void of the reality of Christ's life.

CAUGHT UP TO GOD

How do we overcome this accusing spirit, this devil that seeks to stop the revelation of Christ in our lives? Let us return to the twelfth chapter of Revelation, where we find the key that unlocks our destiny in God. "And she gave birth to a son, a male child, who is to rule all the nations with a rod of iron; and her child was caught up to God and to His throne" (v. 5). As the woman's child "was caught up to God and to His throne," so must we also be "caught up," abiding in the living presence of God Himself.

We cannot allow ourselves to be deterred by the devil's accusation or people's opinions. If the weapon of the accuser is words, know also that our victory is God's Word. He has said that we are His children—that His Son abides within us, bringing us justification, righteousness, holiness, and power.

Since the moment we first came to Christ, there has been an updraft of the Holy Spirit—a constant drawing from God lifting us upward toward the fullness of His presence.

We have seen for ourselves that all things work together for good. We are convinced by our own experience that nothing can separate us from the love of God in Christ Jesus our Lord. (See Romans 8:28, 38–39.) Let us therefore surrender to this wind of God and in adoring obedience allow Him to carry us into our holy future.

It is a most solemn yet joyous truth: the Rapture for which the church awaits has already begun in our spirits! Right now, God has "raised us up with Him, and seated us with Him in the heavenly places in Christ Jesus" (Eph. 2:6)! Did not Jesus say, "I am the resurrection and the life" (John 11:25)? The resurrection, Jesus tells us, is not merely an event; it is a person, and He is within us today—ever renewing and drawing us upward toward the fullness of God!

Satan's strategy is to keep us carnal, religious, and earthbound. But he is too late! For we are, even now, heavenborn and bound for glory. Are we not born again from above? Is it not written that the Jerusalem above is our mother (Gal. 4:26)? Heaven is not merely our destiny; it is our homeland, the place of our birth!

So our first strategy against the accuser is to refuse to allow any words other than the Word of God to define our future. When the accuser attacks, instead of descending to his level of accusation, we must ascend in praise to the height of Christ's exaltation. We flee into the presence of God.

Yes, in the power of Christ's goodness He redeems even the assault of the accuser of the brethren. For it is the accuser that God uses to trouble us toward higher ground. And our God shall continue to reverse the effects of the devil's accusation until we not only come to the throne of God's grace in our need, but also we learn to abide with Christ in heavenly places! This shelter of the Most High God is the place of our destiny, where we are spiritually caught up to God and His throne.

> *Master, how I praise You for Your ability to take even what was meant for evil and use it for my good. Thank You for turning the assault of the accuser into a goad to push me toward Your presence. There is no place I would rather be than secure with You at Your throne.*
>
> *Grant me a humble heart that, even when faced by the accuser, I might quickly flee to You for safety. Amen.*

Arise, shine; for your light has come,

And the glory of the LORD has risen upon you.

For behold, darkness will cover the earth

And deep darkness the peoples;

But the LORD will rise upon you

And His glory will appear upon you.

Nations will come to your light,

And kings to the brightness of your rising.

—Isaiah 60:1–3

TWENTY

ROBED IN HIS GLORY

T HE SPIRIT OF Christ in heaven is the same Spirit of Christ in us. The difference is, in heaven, Jesus is robed in glory; on the earth, He is disguised in our imperfect flesh.

But Christ is the same whether in heaven or in us. Paul makes the source of power and glory in the church very clear. He said, "Test yourselves to see if you are in the faith; examine yourselves! Or do you not recognize this about yourselves, that Jesus Christ is in you—unless indeed you fail the test?" (2 Cor. 13:5).

In another place Paul defined his inner spiritual life as being "crucified with Christ." He continued, "It is no longer I who live, but Christ lives in me; and the life which I now live in the flesh I live by faith in the Son of God, who loved me and gave Himself up for me. I do not nullify the grace of God..." (Gal. 2:20–21).

What is this grace of God? The old, sinful self life we once knew is crucified so that Christ Himself might bring His glory to us. From the beginning, the unwavering purpose of God has been to make man in His image. There is no other plan. God will consummate this plan as the age ends. In Revelation 10:7 we read, "In the days of the voice of the seventh angel, when he is about to sound, then the mystery of God is finished." What is this "mystery of God"? The mystery of God is "Christ in you, the hope of glory" (Col. 1:27).

You see, a time is coming when the mystery of God shall be a mystery no more. Our time of preparation will be complete, and we will be like Him. Our corruptible, mortal lives will put on incorruption, and we will wear immortality like a shining garment. As Christ robed Himself in our imperfect flesh, so shall we be robed in His resplendent glory.

Thus our holy objective is to make way in our hearts for the coming of the Lord. With the vision of God's glory, we pick up our cross, knowing that the sufferings of this present age are themselves being used by God to produce in us an eternal weight of glory far beyond all comparisons! Paul wrote:

> [We are] always carrying about in the body the dying of
> Jesus, so that the life of Jesus also may be manifested in our

body. For we who live are constantly being delivered over to death for Jesus' sake, so that the life of Jesus also may be manifested in our mortal flesh.

—2 Corinthians 4:10–11

The life of Jesus—He is our goal and glory! "It was for this He called you through our gospel, that you may gain the glory of our Lord Jesus Christ" (2 Thess. 2:14).

> From the beginning, the unwavering purpose of God has been to make man in His image. There is no other plan.

Indeed He is coming "to be glorified in His saints on that day, and to be marveled at among all who have believed..." (2 Thess. 1:10). "For you have died and your life is hidden with Christ in God. When Christ, who is our life, is revealed, then you also will be revealed with Him in glory" (Col. 3:3–4). It is this life—the life of Christ—that is the shelter of the Most High God. This is not some "deep teaching," but this is basic Christianity! We are "living epistles," known and read by all men. The church is to be the revelation of Jesus Christ that the world sees! Did not Jesus Himself say, "Father, I desire that they also, whom You have given Me, be with Me where I am, so that they may see My glory" (John 17:24)?

Yet to *see* His glory is but the first stage of *receiving* His very glory into our lives. He also said:

> The glory which You have given Me I have given to them, that they may be one, just as We are one; I in them and You in Me, that they may be perfected in unity, so that the world may know that You sent Me, and loved them, even as You have loved Me.
>
> —John 17:22–23

Our goal is not to tell the world about Christianity but to reveal the glory of Christ. We are not called to imitate Jesus in detached obedience but to actually let Him shine through us to mankind.

Right now there are two persons within every Christian: Jesus and self. Each of us must learn to dwell in Him. Jesus said, "In that day you will know that I am in My Father, and you in Me, and I in you" (John 14:20).

A day is coming, and now is, when the most important truth you can know is that you are in Christ and Christ is in you. "If anyone loves Me, he will keep My word; and My Father will love him, and We will come to him and make Our abode with him" (John 14:23). Our life, once full of rebellion and self-interest, has been set apart to become the abode of God, the dwelling of God in glory.

To Be Known for Knowing Him

In our immaturity we have sought to be known for many things. We sought to make a name for ourselves through our spiritual gifts or doctrinal emphasis. Some sought renown for their type of church government, while others desired recognition through a building or evangelistic program.

Today if we seek renown it must be for this alone: to be known for knowing Christ. His promise is that His presence— His very Spirit and power—will uninhibitedly accompany those who follow only Him. Thus our focus must be on Christ alone; for through Him, God will ultimately accompany our lives with great glory. Yes, great signs and wonders will increasingly flow from our hands, but the miraculous will not distract our gaze from Jesus. For we are not seeking the power of God but the person of God. When our hands are not being laid on the sick, they will be lifted up in worship.

> Our goal is not to tell the world about Christianity but to reveal the glory of Christ, to actually let Him shine through us to mankind.

Thus we find the Holy Spirit directing us continually back to Jesus. Without Him, our prayers are just rituals. Apart from Him, our Christianity can do nothing. But with Him, we enter a stronghold of glory; in His presence we find the shelter of the Most High God.

THE CANOPY OF GLORY

There is a glory coming that will be a source of protection for the saints.

> The LORD will create over the whole area of Mount Zion and over her assemblies a cloud by day, even smoke, and the brightness of a flaming fire by night; for over all the glory will be a canopy. There will be a shelter to give shade from the heat by day, and refuge and protection from the storm and the rain.
>
> —Isaiah 4:5–6

How does this glory come? God is leading the church into a baptism of fire. He has purposed to wash away the "filth of the daughters of Zion" (Isa. 4:4). He has set His heart to purge the "bloodshed of Jerusalem from her midst, by the spirit of judgment and the spirit of burning" (v. 4). The purer we become, the greater the glory that will shine through us; and the greater the glory, the more spacious the shelter of the Most High God.

> *Lord, to know You in Your glory is to dwell forever in the shelter of the Most High. But to know Your glory, I must renounce the "glory" of myself, my denomination, and my culture. You are my glory and the lifter of my head.*
>
> *Baptize me in the light of Your splendor; grant me the grace You granted Moses: a tent of meeting where I may behold Your radiance and beauty. Clothe me in Your presence, and I will ask for nothing more.*

178

I would rather be a doorkeeper in the house of my God

Than dwell in the tents of wickedness.

For the LORD God is a sun and shield;

The LORD will give grace and glory;

No good thing will He withhold

From those who walk uprightly.

O LORD of hosts,

Blessed is the man who trusts in You!

—Psalm 84:10–12, NKJV

TWENTY-ONE

In God's Tabernacle

WE BEGAN THIS book with a warning about the pressures and battles that confront us in our world today. Our hope is that by now we have found our supply of strength in God's shelter alone. Yet Jesus also warned of the deception that would occur at the end of the age. When we consider His words, we instinctively think of false teachers and prophets; these will indeed mislead many. (See Matthew 24.)

But there is another dimension to the enemy's tactics that

is perhaps even more dangerous. We may actually know the truth but be too preoccupied and distracted to obey it. If this is the case, greater judgment will fall on us than on him who did not know God's will at all.

Jesus warned, "Be on guard, so that your hearts will not be weighted down with dissipation and drunkenness and the worries of life, and that day will not come on you suddenly like a trap" (Luke 21:34).

Dissipate means "to fritter away; employ aimlessly; squander; be wasteful." Besides giving us His grace, the second most important gift Christ has given us is time. If we do not have time, we cannot develop spiritually in any of God's other gifts or resources. If we fail to make time for the service of God, we will be unprepared for this day, which Jesus said "will come upon all those who dwell on the face of all the earth" (Luke 21:35). The day of the Lord will not be an occasion of joy; it will come upon you like a trap.

Over and over again the Lord warned that those who put Him off now will be put off by Him later. (See Matthew 24:36–25:46; Luke 13:24–30; John 12:47–48.) They will seek His protection, but He will not provide it. Why? It takes time to grow in the ways, knowledge, and grace of God. It is this very growth that creates within us access to God's shelter. Today is the day to prepare for tomorrow; to wait for tomorrow to ready ourselves will be too late.

IN THE INNER COURT

In the Book of Revelation there is a marvel. John writes:

> Then there was given me a measuring rod like a staff; and someone said, "Get up and measure the temple of God and the altar, and those who worship in it."
>
> —Revelation 11:1

John was commanded to measure the "temple of God." When John's vision came, it should be noted that the physical temple in Jerusalem had been reduced to rubble for more than twenty years. The apostle was not commanded to measure the physical temple, but the spiritual temple. The church is the spiritual temple.

> Today is the day to prepare for tomorrow; to wait for tomorrow to ready ourselves will be too late.

He was told to measure the altar and those who worship in it. In other words, he was commanded to measure those who have presented themselves as living sacrifices to God. These are the souls who have poured out their lives on the altar of sacrifice (Phil. 2:17). They have learned the secret of abiding in the holy place with God.

John was also told, "Leave out the court which is outside the temple and do not measure it, for it has been given to the nations; and they will tread under foot the holy city for forty-two months" (Rev. 11:2).

There are three distinct groups identified to John in this vision: those who worship at God's altar, those immediately outside the temple, and the nations that will tread underfoot the Holy City for three and a half years. In this context, the "nations" represent those who will persecute the unprepared church that was in the court "outside the temple." Those who worship at the altar are those who, through love and perseverance, dwell in the shelter of the Most High at the end of the age.

NEITHER MALE NOR FEMALE, BUT CHRIST

The court that was outside the temple was actually part of the temple grounds and was contained within the wall surrounding the entire temple enclosure. It was called the "court of women and Gentiles." Only the priests, who were male in gender, could serve in the inner courts of God.

This does not mean that women cannot enter the holy place today. It means women must become "sons." (See John 1:12.) To overcome they must crucify reliance on seduction and manipulation, and they must ascend higher than the limitations of jealousy and fear. All these things must go to the cross so that God's Son, Jesus, might come forth in their lives in the true beauty of holiness.

Before the men of the church consider themselves falsely secure, we are not saying women must become like men. No! God forbid! For men also must repent of their rebellion to God, their spiritual irresponsibility, and the multitude of ways by which they express their carnality in games, ambitions, and desires for control.

A son, Paul says, "is neither male nor female" (Gal. 3:28). God's sons are individuals who have literally "clothed [themselves] with Christ" (v. 27). They are fully submitted to Him as their source of identification. They are bold yet meek, free yet slaves, uncompromising in vision yet tolerant toward the weak. To leave the court of women and Gentiles, regardless of one's gender, we must all leave the deception of our flesh nature and enter the presence of God.

> As the age concludes, there will be those who profess Christianity but have never truly taken Christ's commandments, promises, and warnings seriously. They will be found unprepared for God.

In our spirits, we must become "…a holy temple in the Lord…a dwelling of God in the Spirit" (Eph. 2:21–22).

In the last moments of this age there will be those who, although they live on Earth, consciously dwell in the tabernacle of God in heaven. They have made the person of Christ their treasure; where their treasure is, there their heart is also (Matt. 6:21).

And as the age concludes, there will be those who profess Christianity but have never truly taken Christ's commandments, promises, and warnings seriously. When the times of judgment come, they will be found unprepared for God.

I would fail in my service to Christ if I did not warn you of the Master's return and the purity and preparation He requires of His church. Yet He also gives us His unfailing promise: a place of protection, high and secure, full of spiritual authority, and graced with power. The shelter of the Most High is the presence of God; it is found at God's altar by those who worship in it.

> *Lord, how easily distracted I am—how dissipated by the things of this age. Master, I ask this of You: to dwell in Your house all the days of my life, to behold the beauty of the Lord, and to meditate in Your temple.*
>
> *This day I choose to ascend in worship to Your throne. This day I determine to live in view of Your glory. Joyfully, I enter the shelter of the Most High with You. Amen.*

I will lift up my eyes to the mountains;

From where shall my help come?

My help comes from the LORD,

Who made heaven and earth.

He will not allow your foot to slip;

He who keeps you will not slumber.

Behold, He who keeps Israel

Will neither slumber nor sleep.

The LORD is your keeper;

The LORD is your shade on your right hand.

The sun will not smite you by day,

Nor the moon by night.

The LORD will protect you from all evil;

He will keep your soul.

The LORD will guard your going out and your coming in

From this time forth and forever.

—Psalm 121:6–8

CONCLUSION

I T IS WITH reluctance that I conclude this book.

I say "reluctance" because the Bible is brimming with promises of divine protection. What I have provided here is barely an outline. Study for yourself the promises God brings to those who fear Him and to those who walk uprightly with humility and wisdom.

It is from this glorious shelter, the shelter of the Most High God, that we advance. For it is here that we have learned to clothe ourselves with Christ, and Christ is the full armor of God. He is our shelter.